Honour Killing
Dilemma, Ritual, Understanding

AMIR H. JAFRI

OXFORD
UNIVERSITY PRESS

OXFORD

UNIVERSITY PRESS

Great Clarendon Street, Oxford OX2 6DP

Oxford University Press is a department of the University of Oxford.
It furthers the University's objective of excellence in research, scholarship,
and education by publishing worldwide in

Oxford New York

Auckland Cape Town Dar es Salaam Hong Kong Karachi
Kuala Lumpur Madrid Melbourne Mexico City Nairobi
New Delhi Shanghai Taipei Toronto

with offices in

Argentina Austria Brazil Chile Czech Republic France Greece
Guatemala Hungary Italy Japan Poland Portugal Singapore
South Korea Switzerland Turkey Ukraine Vietnam

Oxford is a registered trade mark of Oxford University Press
in the UK and in certain other countries

ISBN 978-0-19-547631-6

Typeset in Adobe Garamond Pro
Printed in Pakistan by
Mehran Printers, Karachi.
Published by
Ameena Saiyid, Oxford University Press
No. 38, Sector 15, Korangi Industrial Area, PO Box 8214
Karachi-74900, Pakistan.

For you, Noonoo

Contents

Preface*

Honour killing is one form of extreme violence perpetrated on women by men. In some parts of Pakistan it is also called *karo kari* (literally: blackened man, blackened woman). It is most commonly a premeditated killing of a girl or woman committed by her brother, father, or combination of male agnates. They do it in the name of restoring their family's honour which, in their view, has been besmirched by the behaviour of the particular woman of their family. The genesis of honour killing in human societies is deeply sedimented in history but has been linked by various scholars with ascendant patriarchal structures. A large number of honour killings are reported from the Mediterranean, Latin American, and certain Muslim societies, but research suggests that it would be an error to view it as being peculiar to a certain geographical area or belief system.

Pakistan is one of the countries where the incidents of honour killing are among the highest in the contemporary world. There have been important scholarly contributions on the concept of honour and how it is behaviourally expressed and understood in various societies—particularly in the Middle East and around the Mediteranean—but little such work has been done in Pakistan. As a hermeneutic study, and borrowing from theorists and philosophers as diverse as Gebser, Foucault, Barthes, Riceour, Kramer, Gramsci, and Spivak, this study contextualizes and analyses the various representative discourses in Pakistan in order to come to an understanding of the possible cultural, religious, and historical reasons that create the exigency for men to kill a female member of their own family. This work looks at this kind of killing as a message, a vivid rhetorical move, in several contexts of Pakistani national life and analyzes how these messages are communicated, and toward what rhetorical ends.

---

*Amir H. Jafri may be contacted at amirj5@hotmail.com

Acknowledgements

This work is an extension of the doctoral dissertation on the topic of honour killing that I defended at the University of Oklahoma in 2003. As is true of dissertations, mine too carried my name but was really a collaborative effort. Deeply woven into that document were the contributions of the members of my committee and numerous academic colleagues. I worked by myself on the transformation of that dissertation into this book, but the fundamental thrust and substance of the text remains the same.

Professors Sandy Ragan and Larry Wieder accompanied me on this journey and provided me with confidence and direction. Their suggestions helped me deal lucidly with the complexities of the subject matter. Professors David Gross and Clemencia Rodriguez often went beyond the call of their duties as committee members and patiently worked with my peculiar ways of making sense of my data. But it really was my advisor, Professor Eric Kramer who, for three years, week after week, sometimes day in and day out, absorbed my frustrations with benign smiles, and occasionally, by tearing his hair out, and who always supplied considered and enlightening responses to my intellectual conundrums. With his guidance, I embarked on a journey to view academic research contextualized within the grand human drama; with his help, I started to become aware of the ubiquitous trap in academia of regional ontologies as limiting impositions. Later, working on this book and with deeper perspective on such matters, I found that understanding to be invaluable.

Earlier, at University of Texas—Pan American, I was fortunate to stumble on Professors George McLemore and Bill Strong who have ever since been stimulating mentors and comforting friends to me. From them I learned to face academic rigors with élan and good cheer. With intellectual insight, unflagging faith, and friendly advice they kept me going when I might otherwise have given up.

There are numerous old and new friends and colleagues here in the United States and in Pakistan who enriched my understanding of the complexity of my subject matter. In the accomplishment of this project, however, I am indebted to Ann Hamilton in a way that makes it almost inappropriate to merely thank her. Over the years, with her alarming facility with computer-related tasks, her lexical rigor, and challenging intellectual probes, she was a constant boon and spur to this project. Without my marathon writing parties at the expense of her hospitality, this project could not have been completed. Alexandra Simou, bibliophile and friend, lent her valuable time and considerable skills with useful suggestions to make this document more readable. I thank her.

My siblings, now spread all over the globe, but never far from each others' concerns, have always been the emotional anchor of my life. It was the love and humour of Anjum, Guddo, Tillo, Abbas, Azra, Nishat, Nigar, Munna, Fatima, Naazo, and a host of other reasonably apprehensive yet optimistic cousins, uncles, and aunts who kept my adrenalin directed towards this project.

This book is dedicated to the memory of my father, Ali Shahzad, who taught me the respect of learning and the learned, and whose exuberant smile at the occasion of this book would have amused our whole family; this book is dedicated to my loving aunt, *Munni Phuppo*, at whose teenage rocking knees, as a toddler, I was first enchanted by the alphabet. Most of all this work is dedicated to Malika, my *maa*, and Nantaara, my *baiti*, my two glittering neighbours on the string of time. Finally, this volume is dedicated to Preeti, who *is* the music on that string of time.

1

Introduction

'All that exists is just and unjust and equally justified in both.'
– Nietzsche[1]

On 6 April 1999, twenty-nine-year-old Samia Sarwar was summarily executed in her lawyer's office located in a bustling business centre of Lahore, Pakistan. Samia had reluctantly agreed to a meeting with her mother and her attorney, Hina Jilani. Mrs Sarwar, Samia's mother, a Western trained gynaecologist, had brought with her a gunman who accomplished the task without much fuss. Samia's father and her maternal uncle were also accomplices to the murder. In spite of the relentless press attention, nobody was arrested. At the time of the murder, Samia's father was the president of his hometown chamber of commerce and a model citizen. Samia was killed because she was alleged to have brought shame to her family and tradition.

A mother of two sons, Samia had been seeking a divorce from her husband Imran, a medical doctor, on grounds of alleged domestic violence and his habitual drug abuse. Having failed to get the divorce through family deliberations, she had sought help from lawyers Hina Jilani and Asma Jahangir, sisters and well-known human rights advocates, who also ran a shelter for battered women. It was during the preparation of legal proceedings by Samia's lawyer for her divorce that the gory drama took place. With this one high-profile incident in the heart of a metropolis, the cultural practice of honour killing—also called *karo kari*[2] in some cases—which had occurred largely without much attention, became a part of Pakistan's national discourse with reverberations across the global media.

If there was anything more shocking than the killing and the *modus operandi* of the act, it was the impunity with which the act was carried out. The perpetrators were not apprehended; they were indeed valorised by organized crowds, by some segments of the press, and by a number of public opinion leaders and politicians. Many social commentators argued in the media that since the killing was in accordance with their tradition it could not be a crime. Some suggested that the parents should have obtained a *jarga*[3] verdict before undertaking the killing to lend it a communal nod (Ziauddin, 8 May 1999). The meta-message here was, of course, that the act was in the natural order of things, and a *jarga* verdict would have ironed out whatever bureaucratic wrinkles may have unnecessarily surfaced. This, in their view, would have made even the ongoing discussion around the legality of the killing moot; for them, the issue was not the premeditated killing of a woman but a procedural oversight by the members of the family.

The criminal case brought against the perpetrators of the killing triggered bitter religio-tribal agitation organized by representatives of certain groups against the lawyers Jilani and Jahangir. In an ironic and seemingly absurd twist, the agitators called for the death of the two advocates for corrupting their women by encouraging them to rebel against tribal customs. The crime, in their view, was committed by Samia; the parents merely committed an act of re-ordination of their universe; they were forced to address the dissonance created by the dishonourable act committed by their daughter. When a resolution against the *ghairat ka qatl* or honour killing was brought before the Pakistan senate, some senators denounced the two activist lawyers for what they thought were their 'modern concepts' of women's rights. Ilyas Bilour, a senator from Samia's home province, asserted that the resolution went against the hallowed custom relating to the place of women and the limits placed on them in their culture. He said: 'We have fought for human rights and civil liberties all our lives but wonder what sort of human rights are being claimed by these girls in jeans' (Verbatim Record of the Proceedings of the Senate, 10 May 1999). His codification of the message in binaries such as tradition vs. modernism, east vs. west, and colonized vs. colonizer was not lost on the majority of the senators who gave him a thunderous applause. The senate could not even manage to pass a resolution presented in a diluted form condemning the incident (*Dawn*, 3 August 1999). Senator Iqbal Haider (9 September 1999), who had tabled the motion in the senate, declared, 'Samia in her death has no doubt become a metaphor for all honour killings. She has become a symbol for all brutalities against women.'

PURPOSE OF THE STUDY

I want to emphasize at the outset that my purpose behind the study of honour killing is not to impose ideologies or to pronounce my judgment on the custom.[4] Neither have I attempted to provide a panacea for social justice or change. While on the one hand I do not wish to be an apologist for people who kill, I also do not intend to view the practice through the prism of one or another ideology in order to establish some kind of ideological ascendancy. The focus shall remain on understanding the cultural and historical reasons that create the exigency for carrying out the act of killing a female member of one's family for the sake of *ghairat* (honour) in Pakistan. Put simply, the purpose is to recreate the context, to bring to the fore the semiotic universe, in which such extreme measures are resorted to.

I must mention here that I am aware of the crimes that are perpetrated in the name of honour killing for a variety of mercenary reasons. According to Shah (as quoted in Amnesty International, September 1999), 'Vested interests … use the excuse of honour as a blanket cover for a multitude of sins' (p. 25). This research is not about the whole 'honour killing industry that has sprung up with a range of stakeholders including tribal people, police administration, and social mediators all seeking a slice of the pie' (Shah, as quoted in Amnesty International, September 1999, p. 25). Most commonly, by projecting the murder as an honour killing, a murderer tries to evade the death penalty or will attempt to avoid paying compensation for the murder, which is required in the tribal system. Often, men who have murdered another man over issues not connected with honour, kill a woman of their own family as an alleged *kari* to the murdered man in order to camouflage the murder as an honour killing. That an innocent woman loses her life does not appear to be of much concern to the murderer who goes on to reap benefits from the ruse. These areas of criminal behaviour are beyond the scope of this work. It is also important to note that crimes of passion, in which lovers or spouses spill blood, are beyond the purview of this study. Those crimes are different from honour killing in which the male agnates of the woman's family consider it their duty to restore their family honour by killing their kinswoman who has acted outside the acceptable code of what is considered honourable behaviour.

To meet the purpose of understanding the custom, I shall explore the discourse that swirled around honour killing in Pakistan during the year following Samia's murder and some of the other cases covered by the media. Another source of my data is interviews that I did with certain people who had been personally involved in the debate. This included some members of the clergy, representatives of human rights organizations, women activists, lawyers, and some plain citizens, the so-called 'man in the street.' Finally, I shall look at some of the Quranic[5] injunctions about the position of women in Islamic society. Difficult as it always would have been, ideally this study should have included interviews with the perpetrators of the crime and/or the family members who have been affected by it. Additionally, an ethnography of court hearings around the killings should have been useful to understand the mindset of the killers, the rhetorical moves, and the atmosphere. Considering the understandable reticence of the individuals in view of the extreme act and the legal and moral ramifications, this is always difficult. A dearth of research in such settings speaks of the difficulties involved. On top of these difficulties, the polarized and volatile political situation in Pakistan effectively snuffed out whatever chances there may have been of carrying out those interviews.

Officially, Pakistan is an Islamic country. An overwhelming majority of the people are Muslims.[6] Many among them do not see any conflict between the teachings of Islam and killing for the sake of their honour. This makes it important to parse the relevant sections of the Quran in order to find and understand the alleged connection. Such an incursion in the relevant texts should provide an understanding of the underlying assumptions in the Pakistani culture about gender, crime, tradition, family, honour, power, and justice. In the context of the present day Islamic Republic of Pakistan, the position and role of women in Islamic society as spelled out by the Quran has a significant relevance to understanding the viewpoint of those who derive the justification of their act from the sacred texts of Islam.

Thus, apart from looking at the contemporary discursive formations (Foucault, 1972) in Pakistan around the instance of Samia's killing in particular and the practice of honour killing in general, I intend to include similar discursive formations in: (a) Islam,[7] as in the religious texts dealing with the view and the role of women in Islamic societies; (b) how these texts have been historically interpreted by whom and to what effect; (c) how the contemporary media in Pakistan viewed and projected the Samia murder in particular and the practice of honour killing in general; and (d) how the representatives of various discourse communities— media, judiciary, clerics, feminists, legislators—viewed the incident; why and how they explain it.

RATIONALE

As heinous as the taking of any human being's life is, in my view there is an exigency about the study and understanding of the premeditated killing of women in the name of honour in Pakistan which is often carried out without consequences. For one thing, as the media reports and the various studies by organizations such as Human Rights Watch (April, September, December 2000) and Amnesty International point out, a surge in such killings during the last few years has signalled the need for renewed attention in the matter.[8] This begs the question whether there has been a rise in instances or whether it is the media that has simply been giving it more attention. Honour killing has been practiced in Pakistan for a long time but had not been openly discussed before—certainly never with the fervour that it is being discussed now. It is important to explore the context in which this change has taken place. There are rules that control what can be talked about at what time, and these rules are necessary for the appearance of objects of discourse

(Foucault 1972), in this case, honour killing. Then there are rules
that silence areas of experience by certain segments of society (often
the disenfranchised) simply by not mentioning or naming them.
The vehemence with which the phenomenon of honour killing has
taken centre stage in the communicative milieu of Pakistan, I argue,
is because vast segments of Pakistani society that existed in the
mythic realm of awareness have come to interface with the mental
or rational realm of awareness.[9]

In all societies particular institutions are recognized as having
the authority to name and define what constitutes crime or what
is 'justifiable' punishment. The word, as is known since antiquity,
is power; (s)he who names it owns it, has power around it.[10]
Nietzsche (1974) underscored the importance of naming things:

> This has given me the greatest trouble and still does: to realize that
> what things *are called* is incomparably more important than what they
> are… It is enough to create new names and estimations and
> probabilities in order to create in the long run new 'things.'(pp.
> 121–2)

'Sexual harassment,' for example, was largely invisible until the
particular conduct was named as such and eventually attempts to
define it were undertaken. 'Affirmative action,' too, is a wrench
thrown in a system in denial about its historical injustices to
disenfranchised and brutalized groups. To understand the discursive
formations built around the practice of honour killing it is
important to consider the voices, the texts, and the knowledge that
have contributed to create and keep the structures of oppression in
place.

It is important to note that only since the naming of the act of
honour killing as such and its discussion in those terms in the
media has the debate been triggered with significant vigour among
the various discursive communities in Pakistan. The term 'honour
killing' though, it must be pointed out, as understood by many is
of the English language and foreign to the 'natives.'[11] In the several
languages and dialects spoken in Pakistan the act of honour killing
has historically been mentioned in ways that directly brand the

victims of the act 'black.'[12] In southern Punjab and Sindh, for example, it is called *karo kari*. Thus, once the *karo* (literally a blackened man) and/or *kari* (a blackened woman) is branded as such—black—an inbuilt finality impregnates the verdict; the word, the naming, automatically creates the exigency of absolving the clan of the stigma.[13] The branding as 'black' implies that the community must be cleansed of the deed that 'blackens' it. In certain parts of the country the sexual act outside of religiously sanctioned ways is automatically called *siyah* (black). The whole notion is inextricably linked with the idea of male *ghairat* (honour). Stigmatizing sexual conduct outside the culturally sanctioned ones, however, is not unique to any one culture but a central organizing principle of most. Indeed, transgressions in the sexual realm inextricably entwined with Eros are the stuff of great literature from antiquity to the present. From Homer to Hawthorne, from Ovid to Waris Shah, poets have tried to express their pathos.

By calling the age-old local ritual 'honour killing' in English the media has stirred up the discussion around the issue nationally and internationally. With this stirring of discussion the act of honour killing has been brought up for scrutiny by women's rights groups. More women have become aware about their rights as human beings. I argue that with the change in naming the act the onus has shifted from the automatically and culturally implied 'blackness' of the act to the 'killing' as a crime. However, according to a report by Amnesty International (1999), if women begin to assert their rights they face more repression and punishment; thus the curve of honour killing has risen parallel to the rise in awareness of rights.

Apologists for honour killing call for immunity to be granted for such acts, claiming respect for customs and traditions of sovereign countries which, in their view, cannot be subjected to scrutiny from the perspective of rights contained in the Declaration of Universal Human Rights or any other such hegemonic and homogenizing principles. On the other hand, human rights activists and feminists argue that cultures are not static but continually changing—increasingly so with the ongoing communication revolution—in response to interactions with other cultures and demands of the modern age. Traditions, in their view, may have emphasized certain norms in the past, but this does not preclude tradition being shaped by new realities. Further, an Amnesty International Report (1999) points out that traditions of honour in Pakistan, which are used to justify violence against women, have undergone change, have broadened in concept and have been debased and distorted by more generalized violence in society. To further complicate matters, honour systems derive from tribal traditions in Pakistan that are often in conflict with other traditions of national life such as religion (Islam) and liberal democracy. This conflict, I argue, is not different from the interface between the mythic and the rational realms of consciousness.

Inevitably, the evolving discourse from these and other points of view continues to hone the concept and weave the moral and legal fabric of Pakistani society. The tensions pulling the possible meanings in a variety of directions are palpable in the national discourse. It is the purpose of this work to explore those tensions and contribute to the understanding of the phenomenon of honour killing in Pakistan.

POLITICAL SCENE

Presently, the culture and society of Pakistan are in the throes of an unprecedented upheaval. In the post 9/11[14] world, the political, religious, and the social dynamics in Pakistan have been under major internal transformation and intense international scrutiny. Ethnic and sectarian violence which ravaged the country for the last two decades has sharply polarized the society. Various Islamic religious groups jostle violently for power. Religious faith, usually a matter of personal redemption, is flagrantly flaunted and a stunning lack of tolerance for difference increasingly defines Pakistani society. In circumstances such as these it is not surprising that ordinary citizens are hesitant to air their views on issues such as honour killing. Indeed, certain religious groups are the most ferocious among the segments of society that have sought through intimidation and threats a certain legitimacy for honour killing in Pakistan.[15]

The so-called Islamic fundamentalists have always been influential in the largely poor, illiterate,[16] and rural Pakistan society. These groups represent a variety of powerful centres based on an array of belief systems from within Islam. Historically, none of these groups have had much success at the ballot box, but with a strong core of 'true believers'[17] with blind faith and unflinching allegiance, they have often been able to display enough street power to disrupt civil life. Since the war of independence in neighbouring Afghanistan in the 1980s, these religious groups have been encouraged and aided by the government of Pakistan and the US State Department. As a result they have flourished and proliferated under the exhilarating notion of *jihad*.[18] The border between Afghanistan and Pakistan has been porous for centuries because of the unusual terrain that facilitates traffic and a common tribal ethos that informs the lives of the bordering populace. With the rapid and fearsome *Talibanization* of Afghanistan and the *Mullahisation*[19] of Pakistan, the borders for all practical and ideological purposes dissolved, and these processes played a vital role in the fluctuating social ethos of Pakistan.

The results of the elections held in Pakistan 10 October 2002 are emblematic of the changing political/religious climate in Pakistan. In the 55-year history of Pakistan, the religious parties had never won more than half a dozen seats in parliament. This time, with strong anti-West sentiment, under the banner of Bin Laden and Mullah Omar's ideology, the religious parties won an unprecedented twenty percent of the seats in the national assembly of 342 and a clear majority in two of the four provinces. These are volatile provinces neighbouring Afghanistan where now they have formed their government. This has been a stunning electoral outcome in the view of most political analysts (see in particular, dawn.com; thefridaytimes.com; and nytimes.com, during October and November 2002).

It is in this context that the discourse around the murder of Samia Sarwar and hundreds of other women in Pakistan on the pretext of honour killing should be viewed in order to derive some understanding of the phenomenon. Honour killing, as will be shown, is not an Islamic custom but one that has often been co-opted as a rallying point by the fundamentalist strain in the Pakistani body politic, meaning those who are considered anti-modernists when viewed through the prism of Western liberal democracy, and by those who, by a range of means, struggle to rid Pakistan of foreign ideological influences. This is the same strain in the Pakistan polity that helped the MMA to its unprecedented success and presently holds the likes of Osama bin Laden[20] and Mullah Omar[21] as its heroes. The surge in media attention to honour killing in Pakistan is just one of the symptoms of fundamental political shifts. That the ritual is becoming more newsworthy speaks to the internal ideological struggles in Pakistan and, at least partly, is the effect of the international gaze on the reported treatment, roles, and rights of women. Again, it can be seen as the encroachment of the mental-rational mode of awareness on the mythic realm.

HONOUR KILLING AS A MESSAGE

Because the purpose of this study is to investigate, extract, study, and interpret messages and how those messages are communicated among the various segments of the society, the study belongs to the communication discipline. On the most fundamental level, honour killing as an act in itself is a message; among other things, it is a dramatic rhetorical assertion communicated by an individual man (or several men) about his personal and collective identity that needs to be parsed in all its complexities. The inability of the enforcing agencies to arrest the audacious perpetrators and the paralysis of the national judicial system to enforce the law are themselves powerful messages sent to fellow-citizens and to the international community about the identity of the state. While a segment of the population perceives the act as pure and simple murder, others view it as an honest and dutiful attempt at the re-ordination of the universe, a re-balancing of the cosmos that can only be made possible by purging a family of profanity and restoring its sacred nature. For those who view it as their sacred duty, killing for the sake of individual and collective honour is not a crime but a heroic act because only under circumstances restored by such killing could an honourable life, the only life worth living, be possible. Thus it is understandable why perpetrators of such killings are considered murderers by some and heroic victims by others. An understanding of the context of honour killing will enable us to answer the central question of this study: How could the same message be interpreted, in such dramatically conflicting ways, by members of the same community?

Killing for the sake of honour in the present context of Pakistan has a communicative function entirely different from how people in the West see it. Just as in certain societies fighting was a game whose rules had to be scrupulously obeyed for all to see in order to avoid dishonour, honour killing is not a clandestine activity but a loud public proclamation in Pakistan. In a magic or mythical world things and people are highly associated, so honour killing is a public display of that strong emotion unlike anonymous drive-by killings in perspectival realms like the US. In collectivistic societies, Bourdieu (1970) concurs, 'the sentiment of honour is lived out openly before other people' (p. 208). In Pakistan, men who are arrested after their act proudly display their handcuffs declaring them to be *marad kaa zaiwar* (man's jewellery); they typically do not go about creating alibis to deny the act. On the contrary, they feel vindicated in living up to what was expected from their manliness as the man-members of the family, by the community; to have achieved merit in the theatre of life 'before the tribunal of public opinion, an institutionalized competition in the course of which are affirmed the values that stand at the very basis of the existence of the group and which assure its preservation' (Bourdieu, 1970, p. 202). This, as mentioned earlier, is a powerful message. The study of such messages is one of the functions of the communication discipline.

RELEVANCE OF THIS STUDY IN THE CONTEMPORARY *ZEITGEIST*

The implications of this study of honour killing in Pakistan for political communication, intercultural communication, international communication, and feminist theory are obvious. Pakistan, with a population of about 140 million people and one of the fastest population growth rates in the world, is a nuclear power and located in a sensitive geo-political space among Russia, China, Afghanistan, Iran, and India. As a wedge political issue in Pakistan, the discourse around honour killing with its overtones of religious and moral jockeying should be an important indicator of Pakistan's political direction. Recently, the president of Pakistan, Pervez Musharraf, personally expressed his dismay and abhorrence of the ritual.[22] It is important to note what kind of messages the evolving political ethos of Pakistan is sending to its own people and to the global community. Besides, study of communication includes an understanding of how and what messages are sent within, between, and among the various cultural strains in a community. The way Pakistan as a state views the act of honour killing is an indicator of the kind of nation it envisions itself to be in the community of nations.

Because of its sensational nature the issue has been amply covered by the media in Pakistan during the last few years. There has also been the occasional BBC documentary, 'Nightline' discussion, a *National Geographic* special, and such Western media coverage that has always, understandably, looked at it from a human rights Western viewpoint reporting about the 'barbarians out there' without really contextualizing. But then such is the nature of news coverage because of time and budgetary constraints. There has been scholarly work on the notion of honour in certain Mediterranean societies like Lebanon, Israel, and Palestine. Serhan (1997), for example, found that several Arab countries maintain penal codes that allow for consideration of honour in murder cases. Examining some of the honour crimes in Lebanon during 1995, Serhan found that the courts take a lenient view towards the killers. Serhan (1997) concluded, 'A hegemonic discourse exists that obscures the reality of the murder, and increases the margin of acceptable justifications for killing a female relative' (p. iv). While studying the construction of male prestige in Israeli-Palestine society, Lang (2000) explored the cultural category of *sharaf* (honour) and its significance in the formation of the male self by elaborating on cultural processes such as family honour killing and *sulha* (an indigenous conflict resolution process). Until now, because of the sensitive nature of the subject and, perhaps, the volatile political situation, scholarly work on honour killing has been scant in Pakistan. This study purports to do that.

STATEMENT OF THE PROBLEM

This study seeks to explore the communicative milieu of Pakistan where men resort to the murder of women in their families to restore the honour of the family. The continuance of the practice is especially intriguing in the face of both state and religious injunctions against bloodletting, the moral indignation among many citizens, the vociferous media outcry, and international human rights laws. Articles 25, 27, 34, 35, and 37 of the Constitution of Pakistan are designed to prevent discrimination against women and to ensure the full protection of law and justice. Similarly, as I shall demonstrate, Islam, the state religion of Pakistan, also provides equal rights to women and condemns violence directed against them. Broadly speaking, how, then, in the face of such religious and legal injunctions, could a killing be openly committed, tolerated, condoned, justified, endorsed, and often applauded in Pakistan?

ORGANIZATION

In Chapter 2, I shall discuss the concept of honour and honour killing through human history. This will include a brief discussion about the way women have been treated in societies since antiquity. I will demonstrate that honour killing is a pre-Islamic practice, the origin of which can only be speculated upon. It is not a religious— much less Islamic—practice but a manifestation of a primal attitude towards women informed by the mythic realm of human consciousness in certain societies. In Chapter 3, I will introduce the theory and method that I will use to understand the practice. Thus a brief discussion of hermeneutics will be followed by an introduction of Kramer's (1997) theory of dimensional accrual/

dissociation, Gebser's (1985) cultural-historical analysis of the various structures of consciousness as they have proceeded from the various mutations, and Foucault on power and discourse.

Chapters 5, 6, and 7 are dedicated to data analyses. In Chapter 4, I discuss certain key concepts—such as pollution, the veil and its association with honour and how it is depicted in Islamic texts, ideals of honourable behaviour for women, and how loss of honour is perceived and communicated in collective settings—that possibly lead to behaviours such as honour killing. For this I look at speeches by religious scholars, interviews that I conducted in Pakistan, and essays and articles by leaders of public opinion. In Chapter 5, I delve into the issue of the rights of the individual and the society relative to one another and how they are played out in individualistic and collectivistic cultures. For this, I use the speeches delivered by Pakistani senators when the resolution to condemn the act of honour killing was tabled. I also parse the data from my interview with a leading feminist lawyer in Lahore, Pakistan, in which she dispels the romantic view that some have about the inbuilt support system that collectivistic cultures have for women. Finally, I look at the relevance of the concepts of 'agency' and 'interruption' as articulated in Western feminist literature and the relevance of these concepts for the Pakistani society.

Chapter 6 contains analyses of the texts of the various discourse communities—the judiciary, feminist, human rights activist, public representative, and the religious—in Pakistan and see how they jostle for hegemony. All these are messages that are sent to the citizenry about the kind of conduct that is expected of them. The judiciary, for example, as a key arm of the state, formulates, articulates, adjudicates, and then enforces laws of the land. The interpretation and implementation of these laws is a beacon for the members of the community; their behaviour is largely shaped by those messages sent as judgments in cases. I also look at the various strands of feminism in Pakistan. For this, I borrow the concepts of hegemony and subaltern from Gramsci (1998). It is also important to note how all of these classes (in the Gramscian sense), whichever side of the debate on honour killing they may articulate, utilize and constantly try to co-opt religious rhetoric.

The statements and texts used from the interviews I conducted are used verbatim and retain the coarse and informal syntax of conversation. When in my view the text becomes too obtuse, I try to contextualize it in order to make it easy for the reader to understand. Usually, I let it play itself out. With help from language dictionaries and thesauri, I personally translated into English those interviews that I conducted in Urdu and the speeches by religious orators that were delivered in a hybrid of Punjabi and Urdu. Similarly, I translated the essays, articles, and opinion pieces from the Urdu press. As in all interpretation and translation work, it is far from *the* final word. But it is *a* final word. I take full responsibility for it. All recordings and texts lie safely in my archives.

NOTES

1. From Nietzsche, *The Birth of Tragedy* (1956), p. 65.
2. *Karo* literally means the black(ened) man in the Sindhi language while *kari* means black (ened) woman. The word used more commonly for 'honour' is *ghairat* (Feroze, S.M.A., 2001, p. 636).
3. *Jarga* in the tribal areas of Pakistan is the quasi-formal assembly of community elders. On matters of individual and collective conduct their word is considered final and binding. According to a paper developed by Pak-German Integrated Rural Development Program (IRDP 1984–90), the notion of *jarga* is of Mongolian origin (meaning 'circle') and has probably established roots in the society during the invasions of the Ephtalites (White Huns) about 1,500 years ago. Principally, it is a council of the elders and leaders of clans, sub-tribes, and tribes. Practically, all community affairs (including decisions about the user rights of common land), both public and private as well as violations of *Pukhtoonwali* (the tribal code) are subject to its jurisdiction. An interesting description is given by Spain (IRDP 1984–90): 'In its operation it is probably the closest thing to Athenian democracy that has existed since the original. It exercises executive, judicial, and legislative (tribal) functions and yet frequently acts as an instrument for arbitration or conciliation' (p. 69 of Spain). Traditionally, a *jarga* meets only at a time of need and has no hierarchical structure and thus it cannot be considered an organization.

4. As a hermeneutist, I think it appropriate, right here in the beginning, to
state that personally I find all forms of blood-letting deplorable and
unacceptable. From the very start I felt a strong charge about the subject
and understood that even when working towards academic ends, I could
not remain neutral, unbiased, or invisible. Thus, instead of feigning
objectivity, I have embraced my cultural ties to what I still think of as
home. I do not stake a claim to be what Locke described as *tabula rasa*,
Gadamer called a 'clean slate,' or Dilthey's ideal of the 'reading-degree-zero;'
and accept the limitations of my Gadamerian 'horizons' imposed on our
understanding not by space but our place in time. I felt the importance of
letting my prejudices, as a representative of a certain tradition, be a part of
what constituted the emerging understanding. At the same time, I tried to
be mindful 'against arbitrary fancies and the limitations imposed by
imperceptible habits of thought' and tried to keep my 'gaze on the things
themselves' (Gadamer, 1998b, p. 672).

5. The Quran is the unalterable holy text that the Prophet of Islam received
over a period of time. Although individual Muslims and Islamic sects
quibble over some interpretations, for more than 1.3 billion Muslims, the
Quran remains the guiding light.

6. According to http://www.islamicpopulation.com, Muslims comprise 97 per
cent of the national population of Pakistan.

7. Islam, the state religion of Pakistan, as I intend to demonstrate, is an
egalitarian and peaceful religion and has absolutely no place for any thing
like *honour killing*s or *qatl* (murder) in the name of *ghairat* (honour) in its
guiding ethos.

8. Citing a February 2003 press release by *Madadgar*, an organization founded
by UNICEF, Cowasjee (9 March 2003) states, 'During the last year in
Sindh, 423 cases of *karo kari* were reported; in Punjab, 319; in Baluchistan
36; while in the North West Frontier Province (NWFP), 45 such cases were
reported in the print media. A comparison of data collected in 2002 and
2001 shows that the trend remains the same and most of the cases were
reported from Sindh. In 2001, the print media reported 453 cases in Sindh
204 in Punjab, 69 in Baluchistan, and 27 in the NWFP.'

9. I borrow this concept of modes of awareness from Gebser (1985) and will
explain it in detail later.

10. The importance of 'word' in the understanding of human affairs is well
summed up by Bakhtin (1986): 'The human sciences—sciences of the
spirit—are philological sciences (as part of and at the same time common
to all of them—the word)' (p. 161).

11. According to Heidegger (1962), 'The Greeks had no word for "language"
they understood this phenomenon "in the first instance" as discourse' (p
209).

12. According to Tresidder (1997), 'Black has almost inescapable symbolism a
the colour of negative forces and unhappy events. It stands for the darknes

of death, ignorance, despair, sorrow and evil (whose Prince of Darkness is Satan.), for inferior levels, or stages (the underworld, primary dissolution in alchemy) and for ominous augury...as the colour of mourning, it dramatizes loss and absence' (p. 26).

13. It may be relevant to note here that according to the Human Rights Commission of Pakistan (2000, April, p. 11), surveys conducted in parts of Pakistan found that men often go unpunished for illicit relationships whereas women are killed on mere rumours of impropriety.

14. For reasons too obvious to enumerate here, since the World Trade Center and Pentagon attacks on 11 September 2001, Pakistan has taken centre-stage in the 'war on terrorism' (see in particular, *Atlantic Monthly*, *The New Yorker*, *The New York Times*, and *Dawn* during the aftermath of the attack).

15. Asma Jahangir, the eminent women's lawyer, for example, said (personal interview, January 9, 2002) a judge and his family were threatened in a case regarding honour killing by representatives of fundamentalist religious groups.

16. According to UNESCO (1998), Pakistan had a literacy rate of 39.8 per cent.

17. I am borrowing the term from Eric Hoffer. Among other things, in Hoffer's (1989) view, true believers see a 'chance to acquire new elements of pride, confidence, hope, and a sense of purpose and worth by an identification with a holy cause' (pp. 12–13).

18. About *jihad*, Tariq Ali's (2002) comments are instructive: 'Contrary to common belief, the concept of jihad as 'holy war' has a limited pedigree. After the early victories of Islam it had been quietly dropped as a mobilizing slogan until revived by Zbigniew Brzezinski in the early 1980s. Brzezinski stood on the Pakistan–Afghan border wearing a Pashtun turban and shouted for the benefit of the TV cameras: 'Go and wage the jihad. Allah is on your side' (p. 20).

19. I use the term *Mullahization* to emphasize the rapid rise of the utopian version of Islam in Pakistan. This movement has been philosophically in league with and chronologically parallel to the *Talibanization* of Afghanistan.

20. Bin Laden is the leader of the Al-Qaida, an extreme fundamentalist Islamic organization, and the alleged mastermind of the WTC bombings on 11 September 2001.

21. Mullah Omar was the leader of the Taliban in Afghanistan. At the time of writing this document it could not be determined if bin Laden and Omar were still alive.

22. Immediately after assuming power in Pakistan, Musharraf expressed his views to Dr Riffat Hasan. Then, as recently as 13 February 2002, on a *National Geographic* special he again addressed the issue.

2

Concepts of Honour

In this chapter I offer an overview of the concept of honour since antiquity in certain societies. Apart from briefly discussing treatment of women in ancient societies, I look at the literature on some Mediterranean societies—mostly Islamic—and the Roman Imperium. This is important because many laws in most of the contemporary societies are inspired by those cultural systems. Because honour is usually associated with the males of a society, the history of patriarchy is an important area to explore in order to come to. an understanding of how violence against women becomes associated with the male sense of honour. Additionally, I parse the concepts of honour and virtue and the way their manifestation shapes societies.

HONOUR KILLING: A BRIEF HISTORY

Lang (2000) considers honour killing as 'most commonly a premeditated murder of a girl or a woman, committed by her brother, father, or combination of male agnates in the name of restoring the family's social reputation' (p. 55). As mentioned earlier, it is in more collectivist societies that killings by male relatives of the woman to restore family honour take place. The assumption is that fidelity and marriage are not a matter between husband and wife, but relate to the family, and that a woman's infidelity—even if unproven—reflects on the honour of the entire family. Additionally, in some cases the tribal council or the *jarga*, as the extended family, decides that the woman should be killed and sends out men to accomplish the task. This bestows further legitimacy and urgency for the act to be carried out.

The practice of honour killing has been prevalent in a number of societies and is not confined to present-day Pakistan, or, as is sometimes misunderstood, Islamic societies. Baker, Gregware, and Cassidy (1999), for example, argue that cultural and personal systems of honour that depend on the behaviour of others are an integral part of the killing of women by the male members of their families. By focusing on honour rationales such as control, feelings of shame, and level of community involvement, men establish such rationales and use honour as a rationale for violence against women, including murder, as was claimed in Samia's case in Pakistan.

Ortner (1978) finds the pattern of family honour evident in Latin American and Mediterranean peasant societies, among nomadic peoples in the Middle East and southwest Asia, and various Indian castes and Chinese elites. In her view, the pattern of family honour and its redemption does not seem to be confined to any particular type of society, or to any consistent stratum. In her study of *sharaf* (honour) killings in Israel, Lang (2000) found that such killings cut across class, ethnic, and religious lines and that Druze, Christians, and Sephardic Jews all perpetrate honour killing. Muslim perpetrators often claim that they were following the tenets of Islam but *sharia* (Islamic law) forbids physical harm to women.[1] It is despite Islam, rather than because of it, that honour killing takes place. Admittedly, in Pakistan (as probably in some other places) sometimes the line between religion and cultural practices is disingenuously blurred by the defence in courts of law. There is a palpable tension between the rule of law and certain social norms. On the one hand, honour defence has absolutely no basis in Pakistan law and Islamic teachings and should be rejected. (Why the judiciary still takes a lenient view of killing for honour is one of the questions this work seeks to explore) On the other hand, tribal customs and social norms weigh in on the man to address the breach in his honour in decisive ways, often by killing women closest to him.

HONOUR

An understanding of the concept of 'honour' is vital for comprehending why men in certain societies address any real or perceived breach in their honour in such extreme fashion. Baker et al., (1999) point out that, 'The conception of honour used to rationalize killings is founded on the notion that a person's honour depends on the behaviour of others and that behaviour, therefore, must be controlled' (p. 165). It follows that other people's behaviour becomes a key component of one's own self-esteem and community regard. It is important to note that this view is different from saying it should be the individual's own behaviour which should be linked with his or her honour.

Schneider (1971) attempts an understanding of honour in terms of power and suggests it should be understood as 'the ideology of the (power) holding group which struggles to define, enlarge, and protect its patrimony in a competitive area' (p. 2). Apart from shoring up the identity of a group, honour defined the group's social boundaries and defended against the claims of competing groups. In Schneider's (1971) view, 'concern for honour arises when the definition of the group is problematic; when social boundaries are difficult to maintain, and internal loyalties are questionable' (p. 2). In collective societies like Pakistan definitions of the group, encroachments of social boundaries and concepts such as loyalty among the kin are of central nature and are naturally linked with notions of honour.

Outlining the social characteristics of homicide for family honour in Arab societies, Kressel (1981) suggests that they are linked to the status and social mobility of patrilineal kin groups. While studying the institutions and moral values in Sarakatsan, Greece, a Christian community, Campbell (1964) found that the qualities required for men and women to be considered 'honourable' contrasted dramatically. For men, honour is a condition of integrity that, if violated accidentally or otherwise, must be responded to at once and with violence if reputation is to survive. The quality required of women in regard to honour is 'shame,' particularly sexual shame. According to Campbell (1964), because honour is always something imputed by others, a woman's honour depends upon the reputation that the community is willing to concede, not upon the evidence of facts. Kandiyoti (1987) concurs that femininity in Islamic society is an ascribed status whereas masculinity is something achieved; masculinity should be seen as a process, something that by definition can never be permanently achieved because the danger of being un-manned is always present through female misbehaviour. In order to protect their shame and their men's honour, women are expected to behave modestly. While the norms and rules about the women's social comportment vary in the various regions they are perceived to have direct effect on men's honour. This is borne out in many incidents of honour killing in Pakistan where sometimes the acts are perpetrated on the slimmest suspicion of shameful conduct on the part of the woman. Significantly, manliness and shame are complementary qualities in relation to honour. The women, thus, must have shame if the manliness of the men is not to be dishonoured.

In Baker's (1999) view, when a female member violates an honour norm, the whole family experiences shame. Thus, Campbell (1964) tells us that killing a wayward woman is seen as an act of purification for the family and sometimes even not doing it quickly enough is perceived to be damaging to the family honour. Ginat (1979, cited in Baker, et al. 1999) notes that in certain Arab societies if a woman brings shame to the family, the man must respond appropriately because by not acting in the expected masculine manner he would add to the shame. In Kandiyoti's (1987) view too, 'Women are vested with immense negative power because any misbehaviour on their part can bring shame and dishonour to the male members of a whole community, lineage or family' (p. 322). Schneider (1971) agrees that the codes of honour and shame are central to the notions of family, historically and immediately. Baker et al., (1999) argue that honour concepts are only another way of understanding the operation of patriarchy which is anchored in the assumption of male authority[2] over women and male definition and expectation of 'appropriate' female behaviour.

Radford (1992) suggests that central to this theory of patriarchy is male sexual violence, a mechanism by which men maintain control over women. In her view 'patriarchal oppression, like other forms of oppression, may manifest itself in legal and economic discrimination, but like all oppressive structures, it is rooted in violence' (Radford 1992, p. 6). This violence often results in what she calls 'femicide' as a form of capital punishment facilitating men in treating women as a sex class and maintaining the patriarchal status quo. Curiously enough, it is often the battered (or killed) woman's behaviour that is scrutinized and blamed when measured against men's idealized constructions of femininity and standards of female behaviour. This collective attitude of honour was clearly in evidence in Pakistan after Samia's murder as it often is. Senator Bilour, addressing an open session of the Pakistan senate, after establishing his family connection with and avuncular fondness for Samia, questioned her conduct and the fate of her killer rather than the other way around. And it is not unique to any part of the world. The male defence, for example, in case of a reported date rape or similar violence often has been a casual 'She asked for it.' Her 'asking' could be a culturally trained and accepted perception anywhere from her perceived gestures to her attire.

According to Mernissi (1987), honour is immediately linked with the family. In collective societies, family is the core unit that the individual identifies with and is naturally a powerful institution in the way communities are organized. In Campbell's (1964) view, in Mediterranean societies, honour is not just important but is the whole worth of the family and it is symbolized in blood. Purity of bloodline bestows honour and this explains the onus on the chastity of women. Once the family honour is tarnished, it becomes imperative on the male members to re-store the honour; blood must be shed. Anthropology literature is replete with connections of honour with family. Minces (1982) suggests that of the community norms sexual purity of women is the most important reflection of a family's reputation. This reputation also has utilitarian functions such as its role in political and economic deals and, more importantly, in expansion of the family through marriages. Honour, thus, is not something achieved individually but is shared; it belongs to the collectivity and transcends time. Not only are the 'honourable' names of fathers and grandfathers on line with the conduct of the present generation but the lives of unborn members also depend on it.

For the analysis of the idea of honour, Friedrich (1977) considers an understanding of 'integrity' or a sense of self as central:

To the degree that such integrity is intact the individual enjoys a sense of wholeness, unity, adequacy, well-formedness and the like. Integrity is symbolized and projected by complex rules of conduct and appropriateness that often go under the label of 'code of honour'. (p. 282)

I argue that in collectivistic cultures that sense of integrity depends on the conduct of the women of the clan. Any perceived breach in that integrity often triggers a violent recourse to feeling re-integrated through the restoration of honour as in honour killing. Friedrich (1977) asserts that while honour consists of a system of symbols, values, and definitions in terms of which phenomena are conceptualized and interpreted, it is a also a code for both interpretation and action, for both 'cognitive and pragmatic components—the second of these components include acts that resolve or terminate conflict and these often have a clearly sexual character' (p.284). This pragmatic component, according to Friedrich (1977) includes acts that 'precipitate or catalyze the normative, 'honourable' behavior that is enjoined by the code' (p. 284).

The notion of honour is of a fundamental importance in collective societies since the dishonourable conduct of an individual reflects upon the rest of the members of the community. In Peristiany's (1970) view, 'One's honour is involved only in particularized relations in which each actor is a well-defined social persona. When the actors are anonymous, honour is not involved' (p. 14). Honour is about the way in which the actor's name is viewed, the actor's own, his father's, his grandfather's, his son's, even his unborn grandson's, indeed the whole family name is inextricably tied with honour. By protecting honour the man projects his family name in the society and raises its capital. In such societies, honour is at the summit of the temporal social values admired. Honour is foundational to the individual's identity. Among the deeds that contribute to honour are compassion, fair play, generosity, courage, effort, and, most importantly, a disdain for death. Perpetrators of honour killing are viewed as victims by fellow members of the community because in their view what the perpetrator had to go through was worse than death, and by doing the deed he displayed courage and lived up to expectations. A folk saying in Pakistan says it all: '*Daulat khonay pur kuch naheen khota, sihat khonay pur kuch kho jaata hai, ghairat khonay pur sub kuch kho jaata hai*' (When wealth is lost nothing is lost; when health is lost something is lost; when honour is lost everything is lost.) Honour, according to Pitt-Rivers (1970), 'provides a nexus between the ideals of a society and their reproduction in the individual through [his] aspiration to personify them. As such, it implies not merely an habitual preference for a given mode of conduct, but the entitlement to a certain treatment in return' (p. 22).

HONOUR AND VIRTUE

Montesquieu's distinction between monarchy, whose operative principle is honour, and republic, whose operative principle is virtue, demonstrates the primal nature of honour and its archaic overtones (as cited by Pitt-Rivers, 1970). The fundamental nature of the difference between 'honour' and 'virtue' is important to note here: Honour is more entrenched, something not intellectually understood but transmitted over generations with subtle behaviours. It is acutely felt and reflexively responded to. The exigency around it is pointed and the immediacy personal, but it permeates the community; virtue has a bureaucratic ring to it, a civic function, something utilitarian, intellectually understood to be of 'use' for the larger good. Virtues such as honesty can be adopted as matters of potentially profitable policy as the English so famously taught humanity. Honour, on the other hand, can never be a policy matter. Its drive is sparked from the marrow of one's existence and, thus, its demands are non-negotiable. As Nietzsche (1974) puts it, 'A man's virtues are called good depending on their probable consequences not for him but for us and society' (p. 92).

The idea of virtue is more modern than that of honour. The idea of virtue is mythic, but in its utilitarian dimension it can be cognitively apprehended; honour and its loss can only be felt. Since possession of virtue imbibes one with a rhetorical force, sophists would work to claim it for their arsenal; honour is more a Socratic ideal.[3] One could be virtuous in a certain matter and not quite so in another or virtuous at a certain time and not so at another. On the other hand, one either has honour or does not have it. Unlike virtue, honour cannot be demonstrated selectively; it informs all conduct. Once lost it resists all claims to being recaptured. If virtuous behaviour can be learned in institutions, a sense of honour can only be imbibed at the feet of elders, from the context of one's lived life, from the animation in the Geertzian webs of significance. In societies that function on strict honour codes, children latch on to the nuances of the social conduct of their elders. Like traffic laws, virtue is something that has been found to serve utilitarian purposes and, as mentioned, like other qualities of efficient citizenship, can be learnt; in modern societies there are institutions where people spend large amounts of money to train to be virtuous, to be able to argue successfully about their virtues. By being virtuous one leads a relatively trouble-free life and may help others lead one too, but by being touchy about honour life can get more life-like: messy. As Nietzsche (1974) says, 'Thus what is really praised when virtues are praised is, first, their instrumental nature and, secondly, the instinct in every virtue that refuses to be held in check by the over-all advantage for the individual himself' (p. 93). This 'advantage' that Nietzsche mentions clearly is not of the mundane kind; it is not of leading a materially profitable life, for example, but entails the realization of one's deepest humanity. This 'advantage' can be attained not by being necessarily virtuous in the civic-minded way but also by yielding to the Dionysus in one. Honour, too, belongs in that realm.

Behaviour can be rationally demonstrated to be virtuous or otherwise. Virtue may be an idea of the mythic, but its use for society forces it to straddle the perspectival too. Honour incontestably belongs to the mythic realm. Virtue is civilized behaviour, an achievement of culture; honour is mired in the primal, in nature.

By this way of parsing the two concepts one sees that a good citizen must be virtuous but may not be honourable. This is obvious from the conduct of a host of elected representatives and legislators and provides fodder for the weekend funnies about lawyers and apparatchiks. The legal framework by which societies function may, on the other hand, not consider the person upholding his 'honour' to be virtuous. There is often a tension, if not an outright conflict, between what is legally acceptable and what may be the compulsions of honourable behaviour. Therein lies the nub of the issue: 'A perfect courtier, he had no moods and no honour,' according to the Duke of Orleans (recounted by Montesquieu, and quoted in Pitt-Rivers, 1970, p.74). An honourable person, thus, sways to the moods rather than weighing the available options and then acting on the most profitable one. Also to note is the difference between honour *felt* and honour *bestowed*. As Pitt-Rivers (1970) points out, 'The qualities needed to exert leadership in a rural community are not those needed to please at court. 'Honour', as a sentiment and mode of conduct, becomes separated from 'honour' as a qualification for the Honours List' (pp. 22–23). Stendhal (quoted in Kapuscinski, 1994) understood the mindset of courtiers too: 'Courtiers of all ages feel one great need: to speak in such a way that they do not say anything' (p. 61). On the other hand, men who kill to restore their honour do 'not say anything.' Spilling publicly the blood of one's daughter, sister, or mother is a resoundingly unambiguous statement. Honour belongs to the mythic while virtue resides in the rational structures of awareness. Honour killing is thus not an isolated message, but an expression of ethos identity and conduct that is etched on the community edifice to be treated. It is a resounding function of interactive communication.

HONOUR KILLING: THE GENESIS

During the last few years, extensive reports have appeared in the Western media about honour killing in places like Pakistan, Jordan,

Bangladesh, Palestine and certain other Islamic countries (see for example, Faqir, 2001). This has led to the belief in the popular imagination that honour killing is somehow related to Islam. If certain Muslims have committed honour killing, or if honour killing has been committed in certain Muslim countries, it does not necessarily follow that it is prescribed, condoned, or tolerated by Islam. As Alessandro Bausani succinctly puts it (in a response to Kressel, 1981),

> Murder of kin on the justification of restoring family honour is frequent not only in Arab Muslim society, but also in other societies, not excluding those, for example, of Sardinia and Sicily. This does not mean that Roman Catholicism encourages it. (p. 153)

Honour killing frequently appears in other cultures such as those of Brazil, Spain, Colombia, and Mexico and has been represented in literary works such as those by Spanish playwright Garcia Lorca and Columbian writer Gabrial Garcia Marquez.[4]

Subjugation, exploitation, and commodification of women are ancient and widespread. The history of human civilization bears witness that women have been humiliated and treated brutally certainly since the rise of city-states—about BC 3600–3100. Women have been viewed as the embodiment of sin, misfortune, disgrace, and shame, and in most societies had hardly any rights or social position. Lang (2000) is explicit about the pervasion of violence against women in general and honour killing in particular: 'Family killings and other violence committed in the name of 'honour' or reputation occur beyond the Arab world and the Middle East; it is by no means endemic to the religion of Islam or tied to any particular group' (p. 55).

There is some research that suggests women were not always so harshly treated. Ahmed (1992) is of the view that the subordination of women in (at least) the ancient Middle East gradually became institutionalized with the rise of urban societies and particularly with the rise of the ancient state. Lerner (1986) informs us that the 'period of the 'establishment of patriarchy'[5] was not one 'event' but a process developing over a period of nearly 2500 years, from approximately BC 3200 to 692' (p. 8). Contrary to certain androcentric theories proposing that the inferior social status of women is based on biology and nature and has existed as long as human beings have, archaeological evidence suggests that women were not always treated with cruelty and that they probably suffered a decline in status with the emergence of urban centres and city-states. There is some evidence of practiced equality at Catal Huyuk, a Neolithic settlement (approximately BC 6000) in Asia Minor, for example, where archaeologists have found elevated women burial platforms hinting at their higher social status. In the same sites, women are also shown hunting alongside men in cave paintings. And as men are buried with their weapons, women are interred with their jewellery in similar pomp. Although evidence from the Catal Huyak settlement is inconclusive about its matriarchal nature, many anthropologists attribute the high status of women to their fecundity, strength, and their role in creating religion at the time. Lerner (1986) concludes that female subordination[6] has not been always present and universal.

Lerner (1986) claims that women have always been part of creating society and of making history but have been deprived of knowing or interpreting history. Not only have women been systematically excluded from the enterprise of creating symbol systems, philosophies, science, and law, more importantly women have been denied any theory-formation. Lerner (1986) calls the tension between women's actual historical experience and their exclusion from interpreting that experience 'the dialectics of women's history' (p. 5). In Lerner's view, it is because of this dialectic that women have made any progress historically. Thus, the dynamic force that propels women to struggle against their conditions lies in the contradiction between their active roles in creating society and their forced marginality in the meaning-giving process.

MALE DOMINATION IN ANTIQUITY

Theories about the advent of harsher patriarchal structures abound. Lerner (1986) suggests that the importance of increasing the population and providing the labour power of evolving city-states led to the commodification of women, whose sexuality and reproductive capacity became the first 'property' for which tribes competed. As a result, a warrior culture, 'naturally' favouring male dominance, emerged. Gradually, Ahmed (1992) surmises, the patriarchal family, designed to guarantee male control of female sexuality, became institutionalized, codified, and upheld by the state. As women's sexuality became designated as the property of men, first of father and then of husband, female sexual purity became negotiable and an economically valuable property; laws became harsher and more restrictive toward women. Ahmed (1992) goes on to tell us that according to the code of Hammurabi (CA 1728–1686) a man could only pawn his wife for a limited time and was specifically forbidden to beat these 'debt-pawns.' Five hundred years later, in Assyrian law (BC 1300), even such protective measures were omitted; explicit permission for violently dealing with the women—'beating debt-pawns' (p. 13)—was granted. According to Kramer (1963), who did archaeological and decipherment work in Sumerian ruins, if a woman 'talked back' to a man, her teeth were crushed with burnt bricks and these bricks, upon which the guilt was inscribed, were hung up on the main gate of the city for everyone to see and to take heed.

Aristotle's views on the place of women in the scheme of things are also relevant since his formulations have to a large extent informed the ethos of the last two millennia. Aristotelian discourse clearly considered women as subordinate by social necessity and also innately and biologically inferior to men in both mental and physical capacities. Following this, he likened the rule of men over women to the rule of 'soul over body, and of the mind and the rational element over the passionate' (quoted in Ahmed, 1992, pp. 28–29). The male, he contended, is by nature superior, and the female inferior; and the one rules and the other is ruled—man's nature is more rounded off and complete. Women, in Aristotle's view, were 'compassionate' but 'more jealous, more querulous, more apt to scold and strike...more vivid of shame and self-respect, more false of speech, more deceptive' (as quoted in Ahmed, 1992, pp. 28–29). In Ahmed's (1992) view, the differences Aristotle discerned in moral and mental universes are paralleled by biological differences. Thus, Aristotle saw female bodies as defective; woman being like an impotent male, for it was, in his view, through a certain incapacity' that the female is female. The female contribution to conception, too, was inferior: Male provides the soul and gives form to the secretion of the female, which merely provides the material mass, in the Aristotelian scheme.

As in other spheres of human understanding, Aristotle's influence in the understanding of gender has been widespread and enduring. Ahmed (1992) states that Aristotle's theories in effect codified and systematized the social values and practices of the Athenian society of the time and continue to reverberate. His theories were presented as objective scientific observations (deductive, as his method was) and, as is widely known, were embraced by both Arab and European civilizations as the articulation of eternal philosophical and scientific verities. Aristotle's opinions, too, have contributed to the way women have been viewed and treated in most cultures of the world during the last two millennia.

HONOUR, WOMEN, AND THE ROMAN IMPERIUM

The notion of honour also played an important part in the structuration of Roman society and the evolution of the Roman law. According to Cohen (1991), historically honour and shame have constrained women from making contact with men because a failure to be so constrained reflected negatively on the men of their families. The first instance of legislating female sexual conduct was in the reign of Augustus (BC 22 to 17 AD) when he created the *lex Julia de adulteries coercendis*. Cantarella (1991) interprets that 'the husband and the father of the adulteress had the *jus occidendi* (the right to kill) only in certain circumstances' (p. 230). These laws provided that under certain circumstances the offended father or the husband could take direct revenge. Prior to these laws, when the state took over, issues of 'misconduct' were dealt with by the father, who under *patria potestas* (paternal power), was given the right of life and death over his children and slaves (Foucault, 1990). The *lex Julia* also made any 'illicit' sexual relationship (as perceived by men about women's behaviour only) open to public trial at the request of any male citizen. Curiously, according to Cohen (1991), the law 'excluded professional prostitutes, actresses, and women who worked in public houses' from its scope. (p. 109)

Since the community judged a man's honour to a significant degree according to the sexual purity of the women to whom he was related, one might deduce that it could be because in the case of women of aforementioned professions the honour of men was not involved. During the Roman imperium issues of honour, shame, and sexual purity were of central concern; we see that statesmen and writers such as Cicero, Seneca, Tacitus, Horace, and Juvenal are on record discussing them. According to Cohen (1991), Seneca considered the lack of female chastity as the greatest evil of his time; Juvenal recommended wives be confined indoors in order to be kept pure; and in Cicero's view the sexual misconduct of a woman brought dishonour to the whole family, the lineage, and to her son's name.

It is important to be mindful of *lex Julia* because as Abu-Odeh (1996) reminds us that most of the later European penal codes are inspired and derived from these Roman edicts. To put things in proper perspective, it would be interesting to note that the lenient view of killing for the sake of honour was removed from the Italian code only in 1981. As Cantarella (1991) sums up, the ideology and the concept of family honour in Italy remained almost unchanged for about two thousand years. During this time, it was used by medieval and modern law to justify a large number of murders. The same law in a variety of nuances is still effective in a lot of societies—like Pakistan—and at least partially explains the lenient view that a lot of judges take of honour killing. Even in Italy, Cantarella (1991) found out that the vestiges of a code of honour still exist in the vulgar use of the term *cornuto* (insult) in legal cases.

A brief look at an aspect of canon law enlightens us about a Christian argument to grant immunity to homicide for the sake of honour. Thomas Aquinas gave the arguments for and against immunity in his *Summa Theologica* (as cited in Cantarella, 1991). One of the arguments in favour of immunity was that because divine law ordained the stoning of the adulteress, the husband who killed his wife was not committing a sin because 'he was carrying out divine law' (Cantarella, 1991, p. 237). An exegesis of the canonical law is beyond the scope of this work, however the fact that Hammurabi, Aristotle, Augustus, Aquinas, and others, were occupied by notions of sexual conduct, honour, and shedding of blood demonstrates that killing for honour transcends space, religion, and time.

As Hussain (quoted in Jasam, 2000) states:

> In all relationships, the most powerful weapon that men wield over women is the notion of 'honour;' prior to her marriage a woman, as a daughter, represents the 'honour' of her father, as sister the 'honour' of her brother, as the beloved the 'honour' of her lover. After marriage, as a wife, she symbolizes the 'honour' of her husband, as a daughter-in-law, the 'honour' of her father-in-law and as a mother she symbolizes the 'honour' of her sons. To protect and preserve the 'honour' of these relationships a woman goes from one sacrifice to another and is repeatedly decimated as a person. At times she is sacrificed for the 'honour' of her man, and at other times for the 'honour' of her family. Ultimately, she comes to signify the 'honour' of her race, her tribe, the land and the nation. Thus when these male collectivities fight against each other, she is the one who must be sacrificed at the altar of male 'honour.' When it comes to the demand of sacrifice, no religion, no sect, no group is different from another. The concept of women as symbol of 'honour' makes them into mere signs in which the actual, flesh and blood woman disappears. (p. 43).

NOTES

1. As discussed in Lang (2000), the Quran (4:15-46) says, 'Those of your women who commit abomination (*faah.isha*) seek against them the testimony of four of your number, and, should they swear, detain the women in their quarters until death release them, or until God appoint a procedure for their case (*lahunna*).' See John Burton for a discussion of the

punishment for sexually illicit behaviour and the bases of the sanctions in the Quran and other sources of Islamic law. Burton traces the debates— origins, positions, and interpretations—of the 'stoning issue' (1990: pp. 123–164) and argues that no direct penal code comes from the Quranic references. In the Quran (24:2) it calls [sic] for stoning adulterers (*thayyibs*) and for one hundred strokes and a year of banishment for non-adulterer fornicators (1990: 127). He points out that the flogging punishment and some references to stoning refer to both male and female (*lahumma*). But other Quranic dictates [4:15] use the term *lahunna* (to her), referring only to the woman. Discrepancies have given rise to *hadiths* and counter-*hadiths* and even claims that these passages refer to pre-Islamic customs (p. 57).

2. In Christianity, for example, this male authority is coded in myths like 'Adam's rib' (Genesis, 2:15–18) and the marriage vows containing life-long obeying clauses only for women. This means, of course, that in the basic social unit of the family, the highest virtues that a woman traditionally aspired for are those of silence, submissiveness, and service.

3. Although I suspect Socrates may argue that honour is the highest virtue.

4. Lorca's famous play 'Blood Wedding' and Gabriel Garcia Marquez' story 'Chronicle of a Death Foretold' both deal with the themes of honour killing.

5. In Lerner's (1986) view, it would be misleading to understand 'patriarchy' as it has been historically derived from the Greek and Roman law, *i.e.*, where the male head had absolute power over the household members. This implies that patriarchy began in classical antiquity and ended in the nineteenth century with the granting of civil rights to women. Lerner points out that since the granting of civil rights, male dominance in the family is being perpetuated by the mutation of its forms. She astutely argues that patriarchy as a system is historical and thus has a beginning in history. And, because it has a history, it can, logically, be terminated by historical process.

6. Again, throughout this work, I use the term 'subordination' as I understand it from Lerner (1986). She, advantageously, distinguishes it from 'oppression.' Subordination does not presuppose an evil intent on the part of the dominant; it leaves room for the possibility of collusion between the dominant and the subordinate in exchange for protection and privilege—a condition that characterizes much of the historical experience of women. Oppression, according to Lerner's distinction *does* imply evil intent.

3

Theory and Method

The information presented in this chapter pertains to the way I plan to go about studying the phenomenon of honour killing. First, I discuss hermeneutics, the science of interpretation, and its centrality to understanding cultural practices such as this. Because Gebser's (1985) theory of shifting structures of consciousness and Kramer's (1997) theory of dimensional accrual/dissociation are recurrent themes in this document, I briefly explain the two frames in the context of honour killing. I borrow from Foucault concepts of 'power' and 'discursive formations' in order to be able to view the jostle for ascendancy in contemporary Pakistani society by the various groups. Finally, I discuss the methods I employed for the generation of data, which include my interviews with representatives of various discourse formations, the printed texts of editorials from magazines and newspapers, and certain governmental and semi-governmental documents from agencies such as Amnesty International and Human Rights Watch Groups.

METHODOLOGY

As has been laid out, the study proposes to explore and understand honour killing, a vivid aspect of Pakistani 'culture.' Culture, as Williams (1985) warns us, is one of the more complicated words in the English language. The ambiguity therein is explained succinctly by Malinowski (1961), who considers culture 'the imponderabilia of actual life' (p.18). Specifically, in the context of honour killing, it may be appropriate to hear Malinowski (1961) on culture:

Here belong such things as the routine of a man's working day, the details of his care of the body, of the manner of taking food and preparing it; the tone of conversational and social life around fires, the existence of strong friendships or hostilities, and of passing sympathies and dislikes between people; the subtle yet unmistakable manner in which personal vanities and ambitions are reflected in the behaviour of the individual and in the emotional reactions of those who surround him. (pp. 19–20)

Admittedly, whatever the provocation, honour killing is not a subtle behaviour, yet it is clearly an expression of one of the intricate ways people make sense of their lives and how certain cultures may be structured. An understanding and interpretation of the discourse around the practice provides a method to better comprehend the phenomenon. Again, in Malinowski's (1961) words, exploring the discursive practices around honour killing should help in 'penetrating the mental attitude expressed in them' (p. 19).

Geertz (1973) argues, along with Weber, that humans are animals suspended in webs of significance they themselves have spun. Geertz (1973) takes 'culture to be those webs, and the analysis of it to be therefore not an experimental science in search of law but an interpretive one in search of meaning' (p. 5). Qualitative methodological approaches lend themselves directly to the study and understanding of the elusive webs of significance related to honour killing. Rather than approaching the phenomenon with the hubris of being able to lay claims to comprehensive explanations followed inevitably by predictions of the behaviour of the people and, eventually, the ability to control their actions, I approach this work with the humility to look at the communicative milieu and make an attempt to interpret the nature of messages being exchanged from my 'limited horizon' (Kramer, 1992, p. 3). As Kramer (1992) warns, 'This is not so much a surrender to nihilistic relativity, but an acknowledgement of the hermeneutic imperative, the apparent paradox of the *law* of being all too human' (p. 2). This is unlike quantitative methods that claim objectivity and are, thus, more suitable to physical sciences. Bakhtin (1998) makes a relevant distinction:

The entire methodological apparatus of the mathematical and natural sciences is directed toward mastery over *mute objects, brute things*, that do not reveal themselves in words, that do not *comment on themselves*. Acquiring knowledge here is not connected with receiving and interpreting words or signs from the object itself under consideration. In the humanities...there arises the specific task of establishing, transmitting and interpreting the words of others (for example the problem of source in the methodology of the historical disciplines) ... In the philological disciplines, the speaking person and his discourse is the fundamental object of investigation. (p. 538)

HERMENEUTICS

Although hermeneutic[1] theories differ from each other across a spectrum, their anchoring premise is the rejection of the notion that reality is wholly independent and autonomous of its explanation. Anderson (1996a, and see also Anderson, 1996b) scans the spectrum:

> At one end, hermeneutics—which posits reality as embedded in world-defining language with its centuries-long history and genetic forbearing, as well as a singularity of application and reference—it is indistinguishable from realism. At the other end, hermeneutics—which posits reality as a polysemic system of meanings that must be centered in improvised performances of both discourse (language in use) and action that themselves are open to rhetorical devices—represents a radically different moral position. (p. 191)

It is the latter that is of consequence in the attempt to understand cultural phenomena such as honour killing in Pakistan. Forsaking the steel-trap explanations and solutions of positivism and determinism, this variety of hermeneutics admits the existence of multiple domains of reality that yield different forms of explanations: 'the brute sense data of physical empiricism is replaced by the necessity of interpretation' (Anderson, 1996a, p. 191). The necessity of interpretation renders redundant the need to explore the material for the fixed relationships of physical causation.

Hermeneutics has an impressive pedigree. As an epistemological and ethical attitude, Kristeva (1998) links interpretation[2] to the Stoics. She cites Epictetus as saying that man is 'born to contemplate God and his works, and not only to contemplate them but also to interpret them [*kai ou monon theatin, ala kai exegetin auton*]' (p. 1076). The act of interpretation in this context means making a connection. The birth of interpretation, in Kristeva's view, is also the birth of semiology. According to Palmer (1969) the provenance of the word hermeneutics lies in the Greek *hermeneuein* (to interpret) and appears in the works of a number of ancient authors such as Xenophon, Plutarch, Euripides, Epicurus, Lucretius, and Longinus. Aristotle's *Peri hermeneias* ('On Interpretation'), too, dealt with the nature of interpretation. Hermeneutics is particularly suited to the understanding of the complex phenomenon of honour killing because before interpreting it one must be mindful of one's own fore-understanding (what Gadamer calls *Vorurteilungen*, 1998a) of the meaning of the texts, and understanding as it goes beyond mere textual interpretation. Hermeneutic theory, in Ricoeur's (1976) view, apart from simply deciphering the layers of meaning in metaphoric and symbolic language or considering the problems of writing and literary composition, should be concerned with the whole problem of discourse. For Ricoeur (1974), 'Discourse is *hermeneia* because a discursive statement is a grasp of the real by meaningful expressions, not a selection of so-called impressions coming from the things themselves' (p. 4). The use of discursive statements surrounding honour killing in an attempt to enhance understanding of the practice is the central method of this work. About this 'understanding' Palmer suggests (1969):

Even for the performance of reading a literary text, the performer must already 'understand' it. This implies explanation; yet here again explanation is grounded in pre-understanding, so that prior to any meaningful explanation, he must enter the horizon of the subject and situation. He must in his own understanding grasp and be grasped by the text. His stance in this encounter, the pre-understanding of the material and situation which he must bring to it, the whole problem, in other words, of the merging of his horizon of understanding with the horizon of understanding which comes to meet him in the text— this is the dynamic complexity of interpretation. (p. 26)

Since the goal of this research is an understanding of honour killing by delving into written and oral texts and not simply to retell the 'facts' but to present them from my (the researcher's) specific perspective, or what Gadamer (1976) calls the 'horizon,' such an approach suits the work. As Gadamer (1976) explains, 'The horizon is the range of vision that includes everything that can be seen from a particular vantage point' (p. 302). Gadamer (1976) argues that since one's consciousness is defined by one's culture one cannot step outside of the culture one inhabits. In the polysemic world of meaning, in his view, objective truth is a chimera. Accepting the impossibility of what a text 'really' means, Gadamer (1976) claims that at best we can achieve an effective historical understanding which, metaphorically speaking, is *Horizonverschmelzung* (fusion of horizons).

DIMENSIONAL ACCRUAL/DISSOCIATION

Kramer's (1997) theory of dimensional accrual/dissociation which seeks to explain communicative encounters in a variety of cultural settings provides a useful frame to understand the phenomenon of honour killing. Kramer (1997) claims, 'The theory of dimensional accrual/dissociation can be used to explain any social behaviour/ communication including other theoretical artifacts, even the bewildering array of other conflicting theories of communication' (p. *xiii*). The theory is based on Kramer's belief that time and space are the two fundamental media, and cultures as complexes of expressed activities are distinguished by variations in spatio-temporal articulations. In Kramer's (1997) words:

> In some cultures space and time is articulated as a point-like unity (the magic world), or as a polarity that is ambiguously defined (the mythic world), or as a sharply demarcated duality (the perspectival world), or

as an integral transparency of identity and difference (the aperspectival world). These variances in spatio/temporal valence are what make cultures different, identifiable. (p. x)

The above four types of expressivities represent different epochs in human civilization and in each, different expressions of the space-time contingent have been dominant. The four types of expressivities include: (a) the univalent which is magic/idolic; (b) the bi-valent which is mythic/symbolic; (c) tri-valent which is perspectival or mental and is signalic-codal; and (d) multi-valent which is aperspectival and is the emergent integral. Kramer (1997) points out, 'As dimensionality increases, so too does dissociation in all its forms, including emotional and semantic detachment from concrete expression' (p. xii).

Since identity is extremely collectivistic in the magic/idolic, the individual is merely a part of an extended family. There is no dissociation or disembodiment or any symbolic distance. As Kramer and Mickunas (1992) put it, 'The magic-vital awareness is one of identity. Every event is vitally connected to and can be transformed into every other event; one can become the other ... accidents, probabilities, and coincidences do not happen here. Things are easily offended' (p. xvii-xviii). Additionally, life and death in the magical or mythical sense are not Cartesian; there is no duality, no split between them. This tendency is manifested even in relatively modern times. Certain Balinese tribes, for example, committed collective suicide by walking into Dutch gunfire (Freeman, 1992, p. 149) or certain Muslims, in order to preserve their way of life or their life or property, embrace *shahadat* (martyrdom), and even today some Hindu widows commit *sati* (self-immolation). *Hara kari*, *seppuku*, suicide bombings—all have the same provenance.

The group/family is fused together through inseparable blood ties. Purity of blood is fiercely guarded. The individual identity is thus subsumed or in Burkean terms 'consubstantiated'[3] in/with that of the group. Because of the degree of congruence between the individual and the group/family, meaning is not only never lost but cannot be misunderstood or misinterpreted; in Kramer's (1997) words, 'In the magic world, there is no semantic space between the expressed and the expression' (p. xiv). I argue that societies/families which take acts like honour killing in stride are predominantly of the magic/idolic and mythic/symbolic realm. Expression is unambiguous. In-built casuistries such as 'deniabilities', 'hedgings' or 'half-measures' are scorned.

Since there is a complete identity between the members in cultures with a dominant magic/idolic dimension, and the identity is not bound by space or time, members are not only inescapably responsible to their immediate family members for the repercussions of their acts but also responsible to their ancestors and progeny for what they do. Positions and roles are prescribed and entrenched; harmony much sought after. In Kramer's (1997) understanding, the prevalence of the caste system in certain societies is one manifestation of the need to maintain specific place. Clearly, the more entrenched such a society is, the more difficult are attempts at reorganizations to dislodge the status quo. Unlike for the perspectival (modern) realm, historical identity, tradition, and context are not bunk for the magic and the mythic realm. On the contrary they constitute the life-world. The magic world, according to Kramer (1997), is 'filled with vital force or energy such as *mana, karma, or chi*. Everything is alive... the world is full of life or 'spirit,' one must be very careful what one does' (p. xiv). I argue that *ghairat*—or honour—in Pakistan society is one such vital force. A tinkering with this volatility by any member of the group/family often triggers an inevitable follow-through; the consequences are hard-wired, so to say, in the culture.

GEBSER

During the course of my study for this project I have not found any trace of a specific historical time or a particular geographical place when men started to kill their family women in order to redeem family honour. The provenance of the practice appears to have been sedimented over the passage of centuries. In my view, the understanding of a phenomenon such as honour killing in Pakistan can be enhanced if viewed through the prism of Gebser's

(1985) consciousness mutation theory. It was during one of my readings of Gebser that I came upon the following stretch dealing with the killing of Clytemnestra by her son, Orestes, a seminal event in human history and one that marks the emergence of what Gebser (1985) calls the mental (or the rational) consciousness in human history. In my view, Orestes' murder of his mother to avenge the betrayal and then killing of his father was an act of honour killing carried out to restore the family honour. According to Gebser (1985):

> The same dread and horror which once overshadowed the mutation from the mythical to the mental, as manifest in the matricide of the *Oresteia*, are amassing throughout the world during our present transitional epoch. It has accomplished patricide and thus sealed the ultimate fate of mental predominance. (p. 425) [4]

It is important to note that in the Oresteian tragedy, the celebrated matricide that in Gebser's (1985) view ushered in the mental mode of consciousness did not obliterate the magical and the mythical modes but superseded them. I argue that honour killing in Pakistan is the manifestation of the mythical mode of awareness. The ascendancy of patriarchy triggered by Clytemnestra's murder straddles both the mythic and the mental perspectives as, in spite of the emerging aperspectival consciousness, the world remains largely patriarchal.

The pivotal nature of the Oresteian tragedy in the history of human consciousness has been pointed out by others, too. Novelist Henry Miller, for example, calls the moment 'one of the navels of the human spirit, the place of attachment to the past and of complete severance too' (p. 68, as quoted in, 1982). Freud (as quoted in Fagles, 1982) considers it 'the decisive step of civilization' (p. 14). Fagles (1982)[5] has variously called the Oresteian tragedy 'a rite of passage from savagery to civilization' (p. 48), an occasion that 'revolutionizes the archaic world' (p. 12), 'more than a rite of passage unrefined, the Oresteia dramatizes our growth from primitive ritual itself to civilized institution' (p. 11), and finally, 'Aeschylus presents our lives not as a painful series of recognitions but as an initiation into stronger states of consciousness' (p. 11).[6]

The event is clearly a shift in structures of awareness. Specifically, in Gebser's (1985) view, a move from the mythical to the mental, which has been described as a civilizing move, that is, a move away from the origin, results in dissociation. This, interestingly, is concomitant with the patriarchal ascendancy, that in spite of the emergence of the aperspectival consciousness structures, holds sway in a variety of ways. As von Salis emphasizes 'History is not a temporal stream and course of events, but a manifestation of interrelated and combined events whose effective interrelationships form it'. (As quoted in Gebser, 1985, p. 432.)

Herein lies the interface where, in my view, the discourse around honour killing has surfaced. As has been mentioned earlier, societies still making sense of their lives by the dominant magic and/or mythic modes of awareness consider the genuine bond between human beings to be sacred, one that is central to the primordial scheme of things. In such societies, blood relationships embody timeless principles of the organic cohesion of various elements of life. These cohesions are violently agitated at the slightest contamination. With the emergence of the perspectival awareness, there is an obliteration of the magnetic centre and the resulting atomism demolishes the ascendancy of the collective over the individual. As Kramer and Ikeda (2001) explain:

> As a person becomes aware of more and more dimensions, that person's identity shifts accordingly. One becomes more and more dissociated from other phenomena in the world. The world increasingly fragments, not only psychologically and interpersonally but also in terms of measurement and mechanism. (p. 37)

Before I suggest my argument, it would be useful to briefly describe Gebser's (1985) paradigm, his universal perception of the world. In his examination of the contemporary structure of reality and his understanding of the emerging consciousness structure, he had identified three earlier shifts in mankind's consciousness development. By 'consciousness structure,' or 'structures of awareness,' Gebser means the perceptions of realities that have emerged throughout human civilizations. The original epoch was the archaic structure from which have emerged the magic, the mythic, and the mental (or rational) structures and the emerging arational.

According to Gebser (1985) 'The decisive and distinguishing characteristic of these epochs is the respective absence or presence of perspective'. (p. 9) The first three epochs, the archaic, the magic (pre-perspectival), and the mythic (un-perspectival), were marked by a lack of perspective. The third, beginning with the Classical Greeks famously discovered perspective, articulated three-dimensional space and has been dominant in Western societies since. This predominantly constitutes the 'perspectival.' And, finally, Gebser argues, is the currently emerging epoch that is the 'aperspectival.'

It is important to note that these emerging perspectives, as described by Gebser (1985), are different from the Darwinian notion of 'evolution' where the preceding stage is obliterated and transformed into a new one. In Gebser's view, we, as human beings, invariably retain elements of magic and mythic structures as we exist in the presently dominant perspectival or mental epoch. This, as I shall demonstrate, is central to a comprehensive understanding of a phenomenon such as honour killing which is informed by mythic ways of making sense of life. The eruption of concern for honour killing in the media and other discursive formations can thus be understood as a manifestation of what Freeman (1992) calls 'a collision of consciousnesses' (p. 149). The recent Taliban,[7] and Al Qaida movements with all their utopian—considered draconian, uncivilized, barbaric by those with dominant mental/rational consciousness—and concomitant instructions like the length of the beards for men and zero tolerance for women's appearance in Afghanistan, Pakistan, and certain other places is an outbreak of mythic consciousness. The Hindu fundamentalist movement in India with the concomitant pyrotechnics of mosque demolitions and the massacre of thousands of Muslims in Gujarat in 2002 is the same resurgence of the mythic. All this is not too different from a similar outbreak of emotion in the churches, homes, and streets of the United States immediately after the events of 9/11.

It is important to note that however hideous we may consider the manifestations of these dormant modes of awareness, inherently there does not exist a 'value' ascendant order among the consciousness structures. This also provides the sharp distinction between the Darwinian idea of evolution and the Gebserian model of dimensional accrual, as Gebser (1985) explains:

> With the unfolding of each consciousness mutation, consciousness increases in intensity; but the concept of evolution, with its continuous development, excludes this discontinuous character of mutation. The unfolding, then, is an enrichment tied, as we shall observe, to a gain in dimensionality; yet it is also an impoverishment because of the increasing remoteness from origin. (p. 41)

Gebser (1985) warns against thinking of this mutational process as a mere succession of events as in the theory of evolution. These shifts in consciousness structures, he explains, are simultaneously incremental and reductive manifestations of inherent predispositions of consciousness, and help determine our understanding of reality 'throughout and beyond the epochs and civilizations' (p. 41). To reiterate, there is no inherent qualitative ascendancy among the various mutations of awareness, yet, as Kramer and Mickunus (1992) warn, 'care must be taken to discern differences among such structures, lest we become subject to unrecognizable forces that can lead to violence' (p. xv). It must be added, however, that in spite of this qualitative non-distinction, we have a propensity to consider the most recent consciousness to be of a greater value. As Keckis (in Gebser, 1985) observes, '[man] has demonstrated at all times the understandable weakness of overestimating and exclusively utilizing the most recent potentialities that manifest themselves in [him]' (p. xx). As an example, he draws our attention toward the current human propensity to subordinate all aspects of life to reason.

A relevant point for the purposes of understanding the phenomenon of honour killing is that in the preperspectival and unperspectival eras people lack individuated self-identity. In Gebser's (1985) view, people belongs 'to a unit, such as a tribe or a communal group, where the emphasis is not yet on the person but on the impersonal, not on the 'I' but on the communal group, the qualitative mode of the collective' (p. 9). This ascendancy of the 'collective' over the 'individual' is of particular relevance for the understanding of honour killing for, I argue, that because the unperspectival (the magic, the mythic) is never obliterated, even when societies shift into the perspectival mode of awareness, dissonance occurs about the role of individuals and their rights and obligations within the collective. Such confusion and conflict is inevitable, given the concomitant disassociation. With a different emphasis, others such as Triandis (1995), Hofstede (2001), and Hall (1969), have also discussed the tension between individualistic and collectivistic cultures.

FOUCAULT AND POWER

Utterances such as Bilour's (see p. 3 of this document) are 'statements' in Foucault's way of looking at communication in a culture. In *Archaeology of Knowledge*, Foucault (1972) considers a 'statement' to be the basic unit of a discursive formation; 'discourse' in his view is the plural of 'statement.' He also makes distinctions among statement, sentence, and proposition. In his conceptualization, while a sentence is governed by grammatical rules and a proposition is governed by rules of logic, a statement is governed by 'epistemological rules.' From this, I take statements (such as the one made by Senator Bilour) to be quarries of meanings waiting to be nudged, cajoled, and released form their linguistic sediment. I understand discursive analysis to be this practice of extracting meaning from such quarries. By 'archaeology' Foucault (1972) means the attempt to reveal:

The stable, almost indestructible system of checks and balances, the irreversible processes, the constant readjustments, the underlying tendencies that gather force, and are then suddenly reversed after centuries of continuity, the movements of accumulation and slow saturation, the great silent, motionless bases that traditional history has covered with a thick layer of events. (p. 3)

In Foucault's (1990) view, power and knowledge—*pouvoir-savoir*—are joined in discourse. Discourse is a series of discontinuous segments, the tactical function of which is neither uniform nor stable. The world of discourse, according to Foucault (1990), must not be seen divided between 'dominant discourse and the dominated one; but as a multiplicity of discursive elements that can come into play in various strategies' (p. 100). Discursive formations surrounding honour killing—those representing the judiciary, women's rights advocates, the media, religious scholars, for example—have varying degrees of dominance that change over time. And these discursive formations transmit, reinforce, and undermine power. Without claiming a hermeneutist's position, Foucault (1990) is doing exactly that—taking a hermeneutist's position:

> It is this distribution that we must reconstruct, with the things said and those concealed, the enunciations required and those forbidden, that it comprises; with the variants and differing and different effects—according to who is speaking, his position of power, the institutional context in which he happens to be situated—that it implies; and with the shifts and reutilizations of identical formulas for contrary objectives that it also includes. Discourses are not once and for all subservient to power or raised up against it, any more than silences are. We must make allowances for the complex and unstable process whereby discourse can be both an instrument and an effect of power, but also a hindrance, a stumbling block, a point of resistance and a starting point for an opposing strategy. Discourse transmits and produces power; it reinforces it, but also undermines and exposes it, renders it fragile and makes it possible to thwart it. (pp. 100–101)

Apart from looking at the contemporary discursive formations in Pakistan around the instance of Samia's murder in particular and the practice of honour killing in general, I intend to include similar discursive formations in: (a) Islam,[8] as in the religious texts dealing with views and roles of women in Islamic societies; (b) how those texts have been historically interpreted; (c) how the contemporary media in Pakistan view and project the Samia murder in particular and the practice of honour killing in general; and (d) how the representatives of various discourse communities—media, judiciary, clerics, feminists, legislators—view the incident.

Borrowing the term *genealogy* from Nietzsche (Foucault, 1972, p. 13) to describe his method of investigation, Foucault expressed his awareness of the importance of power relations to any such enterprise. According to Foss, Foss, and Trapp (1991), 'While archaeology involves the identification of the rules of production and transformation for discourse, genealogy's focus is on the relations of power connected to the discourse' (p. 229). The production and transformation of discourse in its essence is messaging, and thus puts communication at the centre of all understandings. Such a Foucauldian analysis of the horizontal (contemporary) and the vertical (historical) messages sent and responded to by the various discursive formations around the idealized view and treatment of women in Pakistan would be most useful for understanding the phenomenon of honour killing. The identification of rules of production and transformation of messages and the relations of power connected to the various discourses is the task of the communication scholar. This is central to our understanding of honour killing as expressed in various discourses.

DISCURSIVE FORMATIONS

By exploring the messages sent out by the various discursive communities I plan to explore the underlying assumptions about gender, crime, tradition, family, honour, power, and justice in Pakistan. There are a number of questions that need to be addressed in order to zero in on the central (and vexing) question: How can men kill what they most care about for the sake of an abstraction such as honour? Some of the questions that will propel this work are: Is the notion of duty to the family inescapable? Has it always been present? What is the nature of this duty? What legitimizes and justifies the vigilante's restoration of honour? Which interpretations of the Quran by the clergy help perpetuate honour killing ? Are women considered 'dangerous?' How is honour killing different from a crime of passion? What is honourable in this world of modern Pakistan? Was it always like this? From where is the notion derived? In a rather apparent clash of ideologies,[9] what are the various competing strands of the national discourse? Do the instances of honour killing help keep social structures in place? Whose purpose does honour killing serve? What other social implications exist? What norms and traditions (deep structures) in the society under-gird the perpetuation of crimes such as honour killing? How do the rights of the individual and the rights of the collective play out in Pakistani society? What is the role of hegemony in this? Why, for example, has the judiciary been inclined to react conservatively by reconstituting a more traditional version of honour in case of honour killing? How has the fundamentalist agenda come to respond to the complexities, ambiguities, and instabilities of the nationalist project of Pakistan? What is the emergent meaning of gender when the nationalist and the fundamentalist texts intersect? Relatedly, and importantly, are there inconsistencies in the Quranic injunctions and the fundamentalist agenda? Do women have any power in Pakistan? What kind of power do they have? What forces women to subvert their own interests, and, indeed play an active role in perpetuating the practice as Mrs Sarwar did in the murder of her daughter, Samia? Can they, as a subaltern (Spivak, 1998) group, speak? And, finally, if so, how? Admittedly, it will be impossible to adequately respond to all these lines of inquiry within the scope of this work, however, these questions provide a broad paradigm with which to approach the phenomenon of honour killing in Pakistan.

DATA COLLECTION

According to Patton (1990), 'Qualitative methods consist of three kinds of data collection: (1) in-depth open-ended interviews; (2) direct observation; and (3) written documents' (p. 10). Honour killing is not the kind of cultural practice that lends itself easily to participant-observation although, as I had considered, an ethnography of the court proceedings dealing with the crime could have been useful but, in this case, impossible. In Patton's (1990) words, 'we cannot observe situations that preclude the presence of an observer' (p. 278). Another source of rich data could be the interview of the members of the family in which honour killing has taken place. Again, this was not an easily accessible scenario for a variety of fairly obvious reasons. The subject is a culturally sensitive one and poses a number of problems for an outsider. Even if there are internal critiques of certain cultural practices, people generally are wary of outsiders poking around their in-house 'problems.' The palpable hostilities between certain strains of Islam and the Western press further complicate the situation.

INFORMED CONSENT

For the purposes of this study, I conducted in-depth open-ended interviews in Pakistan with people representing a variety of discursive communities. In order to penetrate the collective psyche of the culture on a certain issue, interviewing can be an effective tool to access the perspectives of its representatives. In Patton's (1990) view, 'qualitative interviewing begins with the assumption that the perspective of others is meaningful, knowable, and able to be made explicit' (p. 278). I made a point of informing each of my respondents about the nature and purpose of the interview. In all cases, I made sure the time slot suited their schedules. Their rights were clearly spelled out and their permission was sought to record their narratives and responses on audiocassette; they were told they could stop the interview whenever they felt uncomfortable with the style or drift of the interview. I also assured each one that their identities would not be revealed and that their names would not be used in any way in my work. *Honour killing* is a wedge in the cultural and political milieu of Pakistan and all the people I interviewed were actually insistent that I use their names, publicize the work, and that I provide them with a copy of the finished text. Regardless, no actual identities of the interview participants are used in this document. (See IRB letter, Appendix A).

INTERVIEWS

Typically, tightly structured interview formats are useful for the generation of quantifiable data. Patton (1990) enumerates such advantages as the simplicity and efficiency of data analyses; because the questions and response categories are determined in advance, many answers can be generated in a short time. Responses can be directly compared and easily aggregated. On the other hand, such data can lack depth and can be unrepresentative of the complexity of the world because the interviewees are compelled to fit their feelings and experiences into the research categories. Lacking in flexibility, structured interviews can be perceived as impersonal and mechanistic.

The prime motive behind my choice of unstructured interviewing was to derive better understanding (*verstehen*) and for this I found it critically important to establish rapport with the interviewees. Because I am originally from Pakistan, it was relatively easy for me to empathize with my interviewees. I talked in detail about the project on the phone before actually imposing myself and my equipment on them. In order to elicit information, opinions, and ideas from the interviewees, I decided to let them express themselves freely in a relatively unstructured, open-ended, informal and conversational interview. Heeding Fontana and Frey (2000), I tried to see the situation from their point of view rather than superimpose my preconceptions on them. An unstructured interview, Lofland and Lofland (1995) tell us, 'seeks to discover the informant's experience of a particular topic or situation' (p. 18). Typically, I would talk to the interviewees about the topic I wanted to discuss with them before the interview and provide them with the framework within which we would work during our conversations. Some interviews did spill out of the preset paradigm but such talk is inevitable and may even be useful. Mostly, I let the interviewees sculpt the substance and flow of the interview.

The idea of a specific number of questions did not even occur to me. As Patton (1990) points out, such interviews increase the salience and relevance of questions as the questions emerge in the course of exchange. I also found this conversational mode to be natural and unstilted even if less systematic. Plenty of narrative is generated in such open-ended interviews but on the other hand such data is not amenable to easy coding and quantification. My purpose was different. I was looking for the discourse that articulates the phenomenon and the mode of expression used by various respondents. In my view, the quality of my data depended on the degree of comfort the respondents felt about the freedom to express themselves. I quickly found out that as an interviewer I had to be flexible to the style of each interviewee and be sensitive to the drift of the exchange. Scheurich (1997) warns that interviewing is 'persistently slippery, unstable, and ambiguous from person to person, from situation to situation, from time to time' (p. 62).

I had already read some literature about honour killing in the Pakistani newspapers, magazines, and on the Internet and had had detailed conversations with friends about the phenomenon before I decided to approach the subject for academic purposes. As I mentioned earlier, I am an American citizen but my family and many friends remain in Pakistan. I keep abreast of the political and social happenings there because they affect me in profound ways. During the interviews, I did not flaunt my 'fore-understandings' of the issue, but did not make efforts to hide them or speak around them either. Like Gadamer, I believe that these prejudices through which we interact with texts are not a fixed set of ideas but are themselves constituted and altered by our use of them. I felt the importance of letting my prejudice, as the representative of a certain tradition, be a part of what constituted the emerging understanding. My idea of being an active contributor to the emergent understanding from the interview is not a new one. Ethnographers understand that researchers cannot be altogether invisible but are an integral and active part of the interactions they seek to study. In Schwandt's (1997) view,

> It has become increasingly common in qualitative studies to view the interview as a form of discourse between two or more speakers or as a linguistic event in which the meanings of questions and responses are

y grounded and jointly constructed by the interviewer and
t. (p. 75)

The idea was endorsed by Ithiel de Sola Pool (1957), 'Every
interview…is an interpersonal drama with a developing plot' (p.
193; quoted in Fontana & Frey, 2000, p. 663). The substance of
the interview, in my view, is inexorably entwined with the style
with which it has been conducted. The overall personality of the
interviewer, the context, the situation, the manners, the language
proficiency of both the interviewee and the interviewer, and a host
of other factors affect the emergent meaning. Holstein and
Gubrium (1995) agree with de Sola Pool: 'To say that the interview
is an interpersonal drama with a developing plot is part of a broader
claim that reality is an ongoing, interpretive accomplishment' (p.
16).

Another reason for the interviewer's active involvement in the
interview is the inescapable task of weaving the narratives garnered
not only from the various interviews but also from other resources.
Gubrium and Holstein (1998) suggest, 'The meaning and coherence
of a story is thus drawn as much from such 'narrative linkages,' as
from the disparate items and available plots from which a story is
composed' (p. 166). The interviewer's role thus becomes that of the
thread that holds together the beads of various hues and shapes,
often in dissonance with one another, in order to create a necklace
that is more than the sum of the beauty of the individual beads.
The resultant cohesive narrative, then, should not only incorporate
the individual narratives but also use the national backdrop, the
din and rattle of the streets, and the mood of the people in the
street to contribute to a more comprehensive understanding of the
social phenomena under study.

PUBLISHED TEXTS

Written documents form another source of the data for my work.
In Pakistan there are no university or public libraries housing
archives of the national newspapers or magazines. Computerized
databases are a new technology in Pakistan and as yet not much

has been recorded; usually one can only find the record of the preceding month's issues. I found access to the archives of the premier English language newspaper, *Dawn*, from which I obtained news stories and opinion pieces about honour killing for the year following Samia Sarwar's high profile killing. I found that much was written about the subject and it was difficult to be able to create criteria about the selection on the spot. As a starting point, I simply copied all news stories and editorials published during that year in the hope that as I immersed myself in the material, patterns would emerge. The office of Human Rights Watch Group in Karachi provided me with some relevant print media records that included clippings from the national daily newspapers *The News* and *The Frontier Post*.

While dealing with the written texts, I followed Kincheloe and McLaren (2000) who, while discussing critical hermeneutics, suggest, 'Researchers in the context practice the art by grappling with the text to be understood, telling its story in relation to its contextual dynamics and other texts first to themselves and then to a public audience' (p. 286). As a researcher, I see myself as a bridge between those texts and the reader.

In Schwandt's (1997) view, the importance of the notion of text in qualitative work can be thought of in three related ways: First, Geertz's (1983) extension of text beyond things written on paper, i.e., viewing sentences in a text like moves in a game or performances by actors in a play. This helps the researcher focus attention on how the inscription of action was brought about and what the fixation of meaning implies for sociological interpretation. Geertz (1983) suggests:

> To see social institutions, social customs, social changes as in some sense 'readable' is to alter our whole sense of what such interpretation is and shift it toward modes of thought rather more familiar to the translator, the exegete, or the iconographer than to the test giver, the factor analyst, or the pollster. (p. 31)

Dealing with ancient or esoteric texts, re-inscribing and re-interpreting texts with other texts as a secondary author, according to Geertz (1983), has been the historical role of the philologist.

Second, and in Schwandt's (1997) view, the narrower understanding of text is related to hermeneutics. The text and the interrelated issues of interpretation, language, and meaning in understanding are central to doing hermeneutics. As briefly touched upon earlier, although Heidegger and Gadamer established the idea of an ontological, and thus a universal philosophical hermeneutics, the text remains as the paradigm for philosophical hermeneutics. Ricoeur (1987) is explicit: 'I assume the primary sense of the word 'hermeneutics' concerns the rules required for the interpretation of the written documents of our culture' (p. 197). Ricoeur (1987) also makes a distinction between *Verstehen* (understanding), which relies on the recognition of all kinds of signs in which psychic life expresses itself, and *Auslegung* (interpretation) which covers only those signs whose meanings are fixed by writing.

Since it is as discourse that language is either spoken or written, Ricoeur (1987) posits discourse as a linguistic event, as a counterpart to language systems or linguistic codes; sign being the basic unit of language and sentence (as in Foucault's scheme) the basic unit of discourse. There are other distinctions too: Discourse is always realized temporally whereas the language system is outside of time; while language lacks a subject, discourse is self-referential; the signs in language can only refer to other signs within the same system, discourse refers to a world which it claims to represent. The symbolic function of language is thus actualized in discourse and while 'language' provides codes for communication, it is actually through 'discourse' that messages are exchanged.

A third understanding of text, according to Schwandt (1997), is offered by post-structuralists who hold that life experiences, events, relationships, activities, artifacts—everything—is text. Texts are indeterminate and are sites for an infinite number of interpretations; to borrow Guattari's (1983, as quoted in Murphy, 1997, p. 24) analogy, 'a text, like the rhizome, tolerates the proliferation of new intensities.' Texts, in this view, are related to one another and require rewriting in every encounter by the reader. This is in contrast to the traditional view of text as 'readerly,' i.e., destined for passive readers and read for a specific message. Spivak (1982) claims text has no stable identity, origin, or end. In her view:

> The two readings of the 'same' book show an identity that can only be defined as a difference. The book is not repeatable in its 'identity:' each reading of the book produces a simulacrum of an 'original' that is itself the mark of the shifting and unstable subject that Proust describes, using and being used by a language that is also shifting and unstable. (p. xii)

SUMMARY

In this chapter I discussed briefly the various theories that I will employ in order to make sense of the data about honour killing. The sources of data will be the texts of the interviews that I conducted with the representatives of the various discourse communities during two trips to Pakistan, the published texts of articles and editorials written by leading national writers, transcriptions and oral texts of speeches by religious scholars, records of senate hearings on the issue of honour killing, and judgments by courts in such cases.

The next three chapters are dedicated to data analyses. In the first of these three chapters, after briefly discussing my various trips to Pakistan and the way I gathered data from the various sources, I dwell on certain concepts that recur in the national discourse of Pakistan. And while these concepts do not compel people to commit killings they contribute to a climate in which such acts are tolerated. Following this, I look at the way the Quran stipulates standards of behaviours for women and how these sacred texts are used by religious orators to push their contemporary agenda. Finally, I discuss the role that community plays in communicating to its 'dishonoured' member through the use of *taana* (innuendo etc.) the need to address the exigency.

NOTES

1. Etymologically, 'hermeneutics' comes from the name of the Greek god Hermes who was associated with hidden writings, codes, and mysteries. Historically, hermeneutics is a study of how people interpret encoded texts.

2. *Interpretare*, Kristeva (1998) suggests, is 'to be mutually indebted;' *prêt*: from popular Latin *praestus*, from the classical adverb *praesto*, to be 'close at hand,' 'nearby.' *Praestare* is 'to furnish, to present.'

3. Burke discusses 'consubstantiality' in—among other places—*A Grammar of Motives*.

4. He says, 'with the demand to avoid conceptualizing God' (p. 425). This is a claim that, in my view, has not taken a hold of the global imagination since he wrote it. In this age of exclusivist and sometime alarmingly resurgent fundamentalisms and orthodoxies, the opposite seems to be truer. From the White House to the Tora Bora, conceptualizing God and projecting those conceptualizations upon others with incredibly lethal arsenal is all that is abuzz in this emergent aperspectival (to use Gebser) times. The 10 March 2003 issue of *Newsweek* carried a cover story about the special relationship of President George Bush, the leader of the free world, has with God. Jackson Lears (11 March 2003) under the title 'How war became a crusade' says President Bush, while he was a governor, told a friend: 'I believe God wants me to run for President.'

5. It is important to note that Fagles, writing in 1966, could only anticipate Gebser's (1985) articulation of the pre-perspectival or un-perspectival mode of consciousness as 'archaic'—magical and mythical.

6. Again Fagle's use of the term 'states of consciousness' resonates of Gebserian categories.

7. *Taliban* is the ethnonym that was adopted by the Muslim religious students during their 1980s *jihad* to fight back the Soviet occupation. According to Lane (1956/1885), *Talib* means 'seeking,' 'desiring,' or 'endeavouring to find and to get' or take,' or 'seeker' (p. 1864). In Arabic, as in Urdu, a student is called *Talib-e-Ilm*. The fearsome connotations that have emerged from the literal meanings of *Taliban* (plural of seekers/beggars) are instructive in the way politics and language are symbiotic.

8. Islam, the state religion of Pakistan, as I intend to demonstrate, is an egalitarian and peaceful religion and has absolutely no place for a practice like *honour killing* in its guiding ethos.

9. This, of course, was demonstrated in Pakistan most dramatically in the aftermath of the bizarre turn of international political events in the aftermath of the attacks on World Trade Center on 11 September 2001.

4

Discourse of Pollution

In the previous chapter I had laid out details of the political and cultural circumstances in which data was collected for this study. A discussion of the hermeneutic context facilitates the understanding of the texts. As Mickunas (1994) puts it, one of the fundamental principles employed by hermeneutics is to place the phenomena under study within a cultural field. Having done that, in this and the following two chapters, I present the substance of the various strands of the Pakistan national discourse and parse the various texts to point out the recurrent themes that illuminate honour killing. In the communicative milieu of Pakistan, these themes are messages sent by opinion leaders that permeate the society through the media and to a substantial degree help the community formulate codes of behaviour.

During my first trip to Pakistan (Summer 2001), I interviewed political and social activists, lawyers, academics and others who were articulating the plight of Pakistani women in national and international forums. These interviews were conducted in English, with the occasional informal and inevitable foray into the Pakistani national language, Urdu. Additionally, I collected articles, essays, and editorials about honour killing from the leading English-language daily newspaper, *Dawn*. It is important to mention here the way newspapers are archived in Pakistan and the limitations that method imposes on research of this nature. In order to preserve the substance of the news stories, the editors categorize and then cut (literally—with a pair of scissors) those stories and then, yes, paste (again, literally, with glue) on sturdy paper. They do make sure to scribble the date in the margins. However, and unfortunately for research such as this, the page numbers are never mentioned.

In spite of my best efforts and talking to the chief editor in the hope of accessing the original archive, I had to do with the available resource. There is no 'original' archive; there is no database. I quickly resigned myself to the limitation of the circumstance and moved on (See Appendix B).

On the second trip (Summer 2002), I deliberately chose to interview people who did not speak English and expressed themselves in Urdu or one of the local dialects with which I am familiar. I also collected articles from the Urdu-language press that discussed Samia's killing and the role of feminists and NGOs[1] in the cultural ethos of Pakistan. Finally, I chose several audio recordings of religious preachers in which they discussed the concepts of honour and shame in the light of the teachings of the Quran and *Ahadith*.

In this chapter, I discuss the ways in which certain key ideas connected to honour killing are conceptualized and communicated to the public by some of the influential opinion makers. The influence of mythic discourse on the community cannot be discounted. Some of these messages derive their legitimacy from sacred texts adopted by various communities, playing a powerful role in formulating the standards of behaviour. The senate, for example, is the highest legislative body in Pakistan. In the aftermath of Samia's killing, it failed to pass a resolution condemning the crime. This was a powerful message to the people in Pakistan by the legislators about acceptable behaviour, and to the world at large about the societal model that the senators envision for Pakistan. The minutes of senate hearings, in conjunction with articles, speeches by religious orators, and the interviews are the texts used in the analysis.

In this chapter I explore how, through a mythic discourse, the concept of honour is linked with the behaviour of women, and how notions of idealized conduct are laid out for them by men. I provide examples from texts of speeches in which orators use the Quran to advance their concepts of honour, veil, unclean and polluted, evil, space, gender, honour killing as self-infliction, and the role of community in provoking honour killing.

PREACHERS IN PAKISTAN

In order to understand the power and influence on the socio-cultural landscape of Pakistan, it will be useful to dwell upon the proliferation of religious orators. Qari[2]Abdul Hafeez Faisalabadi,[3] whose speech on the topic 'Veil' I am using for this document, is one of the hundreds of professional religious scholars/orators in Pakistan. They are what in the United States are called fire-and-brimstone preachers and, depending on the occasion, may address audiences of as many as a hundred thousand at one time. Radio and television in Pakistan are part of the state-owned media and usually do not give the religious preachers a free rein. When allowed, such mediated performances are restrained, formal, and less colourful but energized with live audience, their performances often become louder and digressive. I am using one of the live performances. Educated in the proliferating *madrasahs*[4] in Pakistan and well-versed equally in Islamic classical texts and local traditional ones, they are spellbinding orators mixing Arabic, Persian, Urdu, and local dialects with ease and élan. They often improvise and switch easily from exact renditions from the Quran to local apocryphal stories to send powerful messages to their audience.

Some of these orators are very charismatic characters and command huge followings. People seek out their performances for inspiration, and there are stores that specialize in selling cassettes with their recorded speeches. Such homiletics provide articulations for the community—many people rely on these messages in forming their own views of conduct and life. I use a couple of recordings that I bought at a busy market square in Rawalpindi as data in this analysis. These orators most often have a political agenda and make it their business to instruct their audiences and the rulers of the day about the dynamics of statecraft, touching on the major events of their time in the light of their literalist understandings of the Quran and *Ahadith*.[5] Due to political upheavals in the region during the last two decades and the surge of fundamentalism in the Islamic world, the political muscle and influence that these preachers flex has gained unprecedented strength. This phenomenon has become even more vivid now in the post 9/11 world. From the narrow and brute street power that they always wielded, they have gone on to claim electoral legitimacy as mentioned elsewhere in this document.

HONOUR: VEIL AND THE FETISH OF PURITY

Often the preachers give rousing talks about specific topics related to Quranic injunctions or the *Ahadith*. Apart from providing spiritual guidance, Islam lays out a framework for the conduct of daily affairs for its adherents. Therefore, these orators often take on the role of teachers, peppering their lectures with social commentary. As discussed earlier, closely related to the concept of male honour is the idea of female shame. The two—honour and shame—are complementary and enduring social themes in Pakistani society. Among the behavioural expectations that the society has from the women and one that is hammered in by the clergy with sermons is the concept of *chadar aur chaar devaari* (the veil and the four-walls).[6] Not being properly veiled is considered by these preachers to be dishonourable behaviour on the part of women because simply by being exposed to a potentially lustful gaze they can be polluted. Public spaces such as streets and the town square are historically male spaces; women are not supposed to be seen there.

Writing about Moroccan Muslim women, Mernissi (1987) points out that women's use of public spaces is restricted to rare occasions and bound by specific rituals such as the wearing of the veil; only prostitutes and insane women wander freely in the streets. Women in these latter groups are seen either as having lost their honour or as persons for whom honour is not a relevant dimension of their identity. By and large, this claim holds true for all of Pakistani society except in the most urbanized areas.[7] According to Hassan (1994), 'The presence of women in men's space is considered highly dangerous for—as a popular *hadith* states—whenever a man and a woman are alone, *Ash-Shaitan*[8] (the Satan) is bound to be there' (p. 3). In modern Islamic countries, including Pakistan, more and more women are getting educated and working in the public sphere. As a result, they are appearing in public places[9] to go about their business. Custodians of Muslim traditionalism resist this trend as they consider this an encroachment on their concept of the Islamic way of life. The allocation of space to males and females in various cultures communicates the power men wield as a gender group. Of the way division of space becomes emblematic of power in Muslim societies, Mernissi (1987) writes:

> One of the distinctive characteristics of Muslim sexuality is its territoriality, which reflects a specific division of labour and a specific conception of society and power. The territoriality of Muslim sexuality sets patterns of ranks, tasks, and authority. Spatially confined, women were taken care of materially by the men who possessed them, in exchange for total obedience and sexual and reproductive services. The whole system was organized so that the Muslim *ummah* [the worldwide community of Muslims] was actually a society of male citizens who possessed, among other things, the female half of the population ... Muslim men have always had many more rights and privileges than Muslim women, including even the right to kill their women. (pp. 169–170)

The veil is self-effacing to the extent that it renders the veiled anonymous if not altogether erased. Women's presence in male preserves, and the concomitant acknowledgement of their presence, signifies encroachment on male privileges. Such attitudes are still endemic in various societies including some with majority Muslim populations. For men, guarding this privilege of space and ownership is a part of their sense of honour. Sometimes they guard it by spilling blood.

THE VEIL AND POLLUTION

After listening to several recordings of a number of religious orators, I picked a cassette titled *Parda*[10] by Faisalabadi and one titled 'Syeda Aisha' (one of the wives of the Prophet Muhammad (PBUH), and the source of many *ahadith*. She is revered by many sects of Islam) by Syed Abdul Majid Nadeem. Both orations involve themes related to honour. The first speech emphasizes the importance of the veil and the other recounts how honourably certain revered women conducted themselves according to the Quran and *ahadith*. After calming his audience down with conventional preambles such as verses from the Quran, Faisalabadi launches zestfully into the topic: 'The veil is for clean people; the veil is not for the unclean and the polluted;[12] the veil is a sign of greatness, not dishonour; the veil is Islamic and not a fashion statement,' and raising his voice along with the stakes, 'Not the kind [of veil] that certain women take to when going out and display a behaviour which is worse than that of certain animals in heat' (Faisalabadi, 2002).

Women being 'polluted' is a recurring theme in texts produced by various cultures. This idea harks to certain primal notions about what constitutes the sacred and the profane. According to Young (1992),

> The word 'pollution,'[13] one of the most important in the primitive lexicon, points to something essentially bad, even horrible; and yet, because its root meaning is 'a coming into presence of the usually absent divinity,' it also carries an ambiguous shadow, the possibility of a spasm that may kill or cure, or kill as it cures. (p. 232)

The preacher's contortions with disgust at the mere voicing of the word *paleed* (polluted) may be understood in this context. Men who resort to killing women, women perceived to have polluted themselves and the group by acting in traditionally prohibited ways, can also be understood in this light. The killing, the ultimate and complete removal of the woman who has 'polluted' herself and the group with a vile act, is a powerful message communicated to both the ingroup[14] and outgroup members of the community. The polluted woman is literally cast away. Often, the dead body is left to rot in the village square and is not even considered worthy of a proper burial. By not considering the polluted woman to be fit for the traditional burial, the group defines itself and sends a signal to outgroups and to its own present and future members about acceptable limits of behaviour and about what is deemed honourable and what shameful.

According to Jilani (1999, March 21), 'In the rural areas there are special graveyards in which the murdered women are buried as their sinful bodies are not allowed to pollute the resting places of their co-religionists.' According to Amnesty International (1999), a man called Ghulam Nabi killed his daughter and threw her body in a river because he believed she had dishonoured him. Naqvi (1999, October 18) provides an example of a graveyard in rural Sindh reserved especially for those females who were killed in the name of *ghairat*. This *kari* graveyard is a place normal people avoid, because it is meant only for *karis* and, as per common belief, there should be no visitor at the graves of such females. Not even the final rituals—the ablution or the final shrouding—of the killed females are performed.

HONOUR KILLING AS EXPIATION

Some discourses suggest the perpetration of honour killing is an act of self-inflicted expiation, i.e., killing a close female relative leaves a man scarred in profound ways for the rest of his life. In the aftermath of Samia's killing, for example, several social commentators and politicians pointed to the tragic situation of Samia's father. During the senate proceedings about the resolution to condemn Samia's killing, Senator Bilour presented Ghulam Sarwar, Samia's father, as the victim: 'Everything belonging to him has been destroyed, his driver is dead,[15] his daughter is killed, and under Section 302 he stands accused of murder.' To use Young's (1992) terms, a *chaos* (in this case, killing) is committed in order to cleanse the group of the first *chaos*, that of pollution introduced by the conduct perceived as dishonourable—conduct that had polluted the group.

According to Girard (1977), 'All concepts of impurity stem ultimately from the community's fear of a perpetual cycle of violence in its midst (p. 36). Further, primitive societies are more exposed to sudden escalation of violence than societies with more entrenched legal structures. Women's sexual behaviour that is considered to pollute and bring shame to the group is considered a chaos that must be nullified with another chaos. In Girard's view

(1977), 'Blood serves to illustrate the point that the same substance can stain or cleanse, contaminate or purify, drive men to fury and murder or appease their anger and restore them to life' (p. 37).

THE VEIL AND SHAMELESSNESS

Donning the veil is 'proper' conduct for a 'good' woman.[16] Curiously, in his speech on the veil and pollution, Faisalabadi (2002) delivers ample instruction concerning 'modest behaviour' for women, but does not mention any such behaviour standards for men, even though the Quran clearly states that God created man and woman as each other's *libaas* (dress)[17] (Quran 2:87). 'The veil,' he emphasizes 'is for clean women and not for shameless ones, not for those who don't follow the Lord's instructions.' The reason for his speech that day, he informs the audience in rousing tones, is that:

> A flood of shamelessness is at the gates of society. The chief reason for this is the computer. A boy can press a button at his home and will be able to trample the honour of each one of you by accessing your sister or daughter. So watch out for your honour. Get strict about the veil.

Having exhausted the evil that the computer can spawn and the damage that it can inflict on family honour, he takes on the TV/VCR phenomenon and ridicules the hypothetical 'dishonourable' *haji*[18] who has brought a TV and a VCR from his trip to Makkah and enjoys it with his wife and progeny all night. By evoking a scene of orgiastic visual pleasures that the *haji's* family derives from watching 'Indian'[19] movies, Faisalabadi brings the house to a frenzy:

> Curse be upon a *haji* like that; this flood of shamelessness that has taken over the country, your [referring to not only the hypothetical *haji* but also, and more significantly, those in the audience who indulge in such behaviour] wife has drowned in it, your sister has drowned in it, your daughters have drowned in it, your granddaughters have drowned in dishonour and shamelessness.

In a display of stirring rhetoric, Faisalabadi beads the computer, the TV and the VCR, and the Indian movies— significantly all symbols of foreign-ness, hence polluted-ness—on the same string of imported profanity. (The contempt with which Senator Bilour had mentioned the women's rights lawyers as 'girls in jeans' can also be seen within the same cultural frame because 'jeans,' revealing the details of women's bodies, symbolize a foreign pollutant.) Significantly, the preacher's ire is worked only against the (shameful and dishonourable) female members of the *haji* family; the *haji* has been dishonoured not because he was viewing the movies, etc., but because he 'allowed' the women (wife, daughters, granddaughters) to do it.

Faisalabadi (2002), however, stops short of saying explicitly how to handle women who do indulge in shameful and dishonourable behaviour. But the implications have been communicated clearly to the members of the audience by overwhelming the verbal message with vehemence and volume. It is clear that as he invokes the tribal impulses, he is unable to cite any Islamic texts in support. The Quranic injunctions, as has been pointed out, do not support killing or vigilante responses. Faisalabadi (2002) makes apparent that he himself is socially constrained (by the Quran text) and must stop short of herding the frenzied mob to mete out actual punishments to the 'dishonourable.' Regardless, the tribal ethos of rigid self-righteousness and violent retribution has been set in place and by implication—the preacher being an authority on celestial affairs—Quranic approval granted.

Abad, the mullah at the Islamabad mosque whom I interviewed about the concept of honour, was more forthcoming about what actions should be taken against women who do not veil themselves completely and thus walk around public places 'shamelessly.' He stated during an interview, 'If I see them I want to pick them up and take them away' (Abad, personal communication, 22 June 2002).

Because I have walked in those places with the members of my family, I was naturally interested to find out—at least—where he wants to take them. 'Wherever,' he was succinct. 'What for?' I insisted. 'Whatever may be the purpose, I just want to cut them into bits or betroth[20] them to someone but I feel helpless. When you take away a girl like that once, next day no other girl will come for a walk.' Startled, I asked him if Islam, the religion of order and peace endorses that. He blushed in a moment of silence and then, chin up with self-righteous pride, looked around at his protégés, and mumbled audibly: 'Islam does not allow it but sometimes you have to do it to set an example.' Clearly, at that eloquent communicative moment, his immediate audience had changed: the audience was no longer me, but his protégés. It appeared he was compelled to bring his message in line with what he usually taught them.

Siddiqui (1999, June) also recognizes the entwined relationship of the veil and honour. In his view, 'Westerners cannot empathize with the sense of loss of honour that men in our culture are capable of experiencing because thousands of years of *bay purdigi*[21] has tarnished their sense of honour' (p. 49). This loss of honour is experienced by men in certain cultures because 'in its essence, the honour of men is the same as their women's chastity, and the survival of the family institution wholly depends on it' (p. 48). As discussed earlier, Gebser (1985) designates such cultures as predominantly magic/mythic structures of consciousness, a state in which man lacks self-identity. According to Gebser (1985), in this state man 'belongs to a unit, such as a tribe or communal group, where the emphasis is not yet on the person but on the impersonal, not on the "I" but on the communal group, the qualitative mode of the collective' (p. 9). The sense of honour in men seems to be directly related to their identification with their tribe, family, or communal group. Siddiqui (1999, June) claims that there is no distance between a woman's chastity and a man's honour; it constitutes the same hyper-cohesive unit. To use Kramer's (1997) word, the magic world is 'full' (p. xiv).

Discussing the complementary relationship between 'honour' and 'value,' Shah (19 November 1998) claims that although honour is an abstract principle it resides in an object of value. She does not specify that it is abstract only to the perspectival, the mental mode of consciousness and not for the magic or mythic. In her opinion, 'A man's property, wealth, and all that is linked with these is the sum total of his honour value. A woman is also an object of value in tribal societies in the world. Honour is, therefore, a male value derived and viewed against the index of a woman's body.' In Kramer's (1997) view, 'Magic identity is collectivistic to the extreme. Who am I? I am part of an extended family'. (p. xiii) The sense of honour is the glue that keeps the collective nature of society intact by being prickly about what it values. Honour is a mythic construct. Societies have fables and tales that congeal the individual's concept about it. There are elaborate rules of conduct around hierarchies and genders that are not laid out in specific language but are deeply understood. Good and evil are not disputable. In Kramer's (1997) words, 'The magic world is a womb of belonging and sharing where blood ties take precedence over all other criteria' (p. xiii). Conduct that in any way infringes upon the collective, the sense of honour, has to be corrected. Sometime this results in killings for the restoration of personal or family honour. For men who communicate in the magic/idolic, honour killing, the spilling of their own blood, though it runs in someone else's veins, is the unleashing of a 'vital force' (Kramer 1997, p. xiv). The duty to address shame is inescapable because men consider their women's 'shame' as their own; the familial ties cannot be broken. The rites must be performed.

GHAIRAT (HONOUR) AS A TRIBAL NOTION

Husain (17 April 1999), along with numerous others mentioned, also suggests there is no place in Islam for killing in the name of *ghairat*. Instead he ties it to a deficient tribal mode of life:

> The whole concept of *ghairat* is based on a tribal, pre-Islamic worldview in which woman is considered as chattel with no mind or will of her own. Islam came as a liberating force, conferring rights on women that were unheard of in those days. Unfortunately, in the more retrograde parts of the Muslim world, these rights have been snatched away in the name of honour that has been accorded a false stamp of orthodoxy.

What Husain (1999, April 17) calls the 'tribal, pre-Islamic worldview' and his view of Islam as the forward-looking 'liberating force' is akin to the mythic and the mental worlds, the unperspectival and the perspectival, respectively. The killing of kinswomen in response to perceived breaches of honour clearly finds no endorsement from the relatively rationalistic Islamic texts but seeks inspiration from the more primal codes. Honour killing may occur in certain Islamic societies but such killing is not confined to these societies. There is tension between tribal and the Islamic discourses about honour killing, the latter unable to completely overwhelm the former, just as the magic (or the mythic) world can never be totally obliterated by the mental, and surfaces in cathartic times. An example is the return to religious rituals during catastrophes like wars and natural calamities, and celebrations such as marriages and births.

Shahid, (12 April 1999) also connects the notion of *ghairat* with tribal and feudal traditions and not with Islamic injunctions. Additionally, he equates *ghairat* with lack of education, an epitome of the perspectival world: 'We live in one of the most traditional, conservative societies in the world … religious fundamentalism is very strong in the country … men tend to develop an unhealthy sense of *ghairat*—especially in backward areas and among uneducated sections of society.' By 'education' Shahid implies the process of understanding the 'Enlightenment' project, of being able to be critical thinkers, to be able to develop a fundamentally different 'ecology of the mind' (Kramer & Ikeda, 2001, p. 40), and to be able to 'rationally' think things through. This training represents the mental realm, as described by Gebser (1985). According to Kramer (1997), for magic people (what Shahid, , 12 April 1999 calls 'tribal') notions like progress and development are profane because they consider themselves complete. What Shahid considers 'unhealthy sense of *ghairat*' is for them a critical aspect of their being 'full' (Kramer, 1997, p. xiv). They are not (yet) equipped with the dissociative distance from their defining aspects—like honour killing—to be able to develop reflective consciousness. Until then, any infringement in the way the people of the magic/mythic world make sense of their world would unsettle them, scatter their cosmos. Reacting violently to a suddenly disarrayed cosmos may not be something we endorse—nor does Islam—but, in its context, violence—in this case, honour killing—begs understanding.

The connection of the veil to *ghairat* was also emphasized by Bakram (personal communication, 9 July 2002). A retired police official, he was a regular at the same mosque in Islamabad at which Abad is the resident mullah. I interviewed him at a different time and place. When asked what it means to be *bay-ghairat* (the one without honour), he said:

> If you go to Bannu you will see that no woman comes out. Now women have started to work in Lahore, 'Pindi, and Karachi ... but our Muslim tribal people do not let our women out. If they do, they wear a veil with a cap with fine holes to look out but from which her face cannot be seen and she has gloves on her hands and feet so that no one can see any part of her body. This is what we call honour.

STANDARDS OF WOMEN'S CONDUCT AND THE QURAN

In order to set the standard for honourable behaviour by women, Faisalabadi (2002) recalls *Surah* 19 from the Quran, called *Surah Maryam*. As an example of honourable behaviour by women, he says, Maryam (*Mary*) resisted the archangel Gabriel who on God's command had appeared in her sleeping chambers as a 'perfect man.' Earlier Gabriel had a dialogue with God in which he argued against women who, in his view, were nothing but trouble. As is well known, Gabriel, as God's messenger, was on duty instructing Mary about the Lord's plan for the immaculate conception. After this most famous birth in history, Mary brought Jesus to her town square where she had to face her questioning tribe about the uncommon circumstance of the child's birth.

Here, Faisalabadi (2002) works up the emotions of the audience by embellishing the Quranic text in an effort to support the tribal ethos with the sacred injunction. Before proceeding to the town square, he has Mary grovelling to God in the singsong folk-tale

narrative traditional style of Pakistan; for rhetorical effect, he
contemporizes, localizes, and personalizes the mythological figures
of God, Mary, Gabriel, and Jesus: 'Oh my dear God, now that I
have become a virgin mother who will believe me? Who will
provide evidence for us, the lowly? Oh God, when I take this child
to the town square people from my tribe will hack me to pieces.'
In order to sell the idea of the veil to his audience, Faisalabadi
(2002), then has God assuring Mary:

> Oh Mary, why have you become nervous? During your life you had
> made the veil and shame your jewels for my sake. How can I not
> protect you? I would have the innocent one [Jesus] be your witness. I
> will mention you in the Old Testament, in the New Testament, and
> the Quran. Your veil and shame will live as long as there is life.

There is no ambiguity in the Quran or any other religious text
about Mary's innocence and conduct, and the interpolation of the
veil and God's positioning of the veil on the highest pedestal of
female conduct is a pure weave of mythology. As Barthes (1989)
explains, 'However paradoxical it may seem, *myth hides nothing*: its
function is to distort not to make disappear ... the relation which
unites the concept of the myth to its meaning is essentially a
relation of *deformation*' (pp. 121–122, emphasis in original).

First, the Old Testament was already revealed at the time of
Mary's crisis so that may have been either a slip or a rhetorical
excess on Faisalabadi's part. I read the chapter and verse of *Surah
Maryam* thoroughly in Arabic and in English. Additionally, I also
took the text to the sheikh of the local mosque and discussed it
with him and his colleagues. There is no mention of such dialogue
or such theatrical language between Mary and God in the text.
According to the Quran, after the birth of Jesus, Mary takes some
rest, and then, with the infant in her arms, proceeds to the town
square. There is no grovelling on Mary's part nor paeans to the veil
and shame by God in the interim in the text. Concern with such
rhetorical flourishes is immaterial. As Barthes (1989) points out,
'Myth hides nothing and flaunts nothing: it distorts; myth is
neither a lie nor a confession: it is an inflexion' (p. 128).

Faced with the hostile fellow tribesmen at the town square, according to Faisalabadi, Mary was at her wit's end. At that moment, in Faisalabadi's story, God instructed the infant Jesus to take over. In immaculate Arabic, thus spoke the infant Jesus: 'I am the slave of Allah. He hath given me the Scripture and hath appointed me a prophet.' Naturally, everyone present was stunned and the rest, as they say, is history and stuff that faiths are made of. Here the Quranic narrative veers into a related direction, but, finding the audience charged, Faisalabadi moves on for a grand denouement of the epic drama by declaring that the infant Jesus (also) said: 'Oh you accusers of my mother, do you know that my mother has made shame into Quran? She has made the idea of the veil and shame into Quran.'[22] This is clearly not a slip. This is an astonishing leap. At the risk of sounding like a mullah myself, I am tempted to call it sacrilegious. Jesus, as everyone knows was born more that 600 years before the Quran was revealed. The moral that Faisalabadi (2002) derives from this narration is that if our women will fulfil the requirements of the *chadar aur chaar devaari*, that is, if they will veil themselves properly, they too will be successful in this life and on the day of Judgment, and if their conduct has been honourable God Himself will come and bear witness to their honourable behaviour. The Quran does not say it but Faisalabadi clearly implies that in the case of an accusation of breaching a man's honour, a woman is guilty until divine intervention, as in the case of Mary, rescues her.

A message is being sent to the community, especially the women, with the invocation of myth and use of simile and hyperbole. A utilitarian matrix is created to lay down the ideals of women's conduct in society. By presenting worldly peace and afterlife redemptions as incentives, the hegemonic discourse attempts to prevent any potential subversion. An incident in a revered text is utilized to define the community's concept of good and evil. History and chronology are thus rendered irrelevant and universalism projected in all directions. As an example of mythic discourse, it articulates the community's shared values and warns about the dangers of potential conflict that may arise from deviant behaviour. The story retains its spirit but is transmuted into another context and language to relay a specific social message. The medium and the context are part of the message. This is not a religious sermon as Faisalabadi would have his audience believe, but a mythical narrative as he does not follow the sacred text.[23] This mythologizing on Faisalabadi's part is called *zeb-e-daastaan* (decorating the folk tale) in Urdu. As Barthes (1989) explains,

> Mythical speech is made of a material which has *already* been worked on so as to make it suitable for communication: it is because all the materials of myth (whether pictorial or written) presuppose a signifying consciousness that one can reason about them while discounting their substance. (p. 110)

By and large, Faisalabadi's audience is well versed in the literal text of the Quran and he knows it well; so by weaving a yarn around it, Faisalabadi is creating a persuasive message about the specific mores of the time in Pakistani society. By pointing out the essentials of the text and deriving from them the lessons for contemporary notions of conduct and behaviour, Faisalabadi (2002) elucidates his own understanding and imposes it on his audience.

FITNA AND THE CONCOMITANT CHAOS

The concept of *fitna*[24] is important to dwell on here, too. In the texts dealing with the phenomenon of honour killing, sometimes it appears literally for the destructive powers that women have and sometimes as a metaphor for women's behaviour that is considered dishonourable. But *fitna* is a word with a variety of meanings all of which imply disruption to peace of mind and social stability. *Fitna* also represents forces that can unleash uncontrollable social chaos. *Fitna* partakes of the Dionysian. Thus it is interesting that it is sometimes identified with women by poets and preachers. Stillman (personal communication, 27 February 2003) acknowledges the rich variety of ways it can be used but considers it to be essentially representative of 'dissension.' The period of Islamic history immediately following the prophet's death, when for some time chaos reigned is called the period of *fitna*. Then the period of unrest in Islamic Spain between 1009 and 1090 is also considered a period of *fitna*. As a more immediate example, Stillman (personal communication, 27 February 2003) mentioned his experience in Morocco in 1971 when there was a failed uprising against King Hasan. After successfully pre-empting the attempt to overthrow him, Hasan addressed his nation in coarse Arabic and declared that he would not tolerate *fitna*. *Fitna* has the ability to awaken the dormant but ever-present Dionysus.

According to the index to the Quran (Abdul Baqi, 1945), the word *fitna* appears thirty times and another twenty-three times as other words derived from it in the total one hundred and fourteen *surahs* of the Quran. The word is never used directly to stigmatize women in the text. In most places, it refers to the temptations of life: *fitna* can be sparked by lust for power, money, grandeur, worldly possessions. For the righteous men, therefore, women, children, and other worldly pleasures, can be temptations (Quran 64:15). Magic, of which *fitna* partakes, is seductive and, tinged with it, life can be intoxicating. According to the Quran (1:6) [25] the true purpose of existence is the *siraat ul mustaqeem* (the right path) and those (people, objects, desires, etc.) that we love in life have the ability to distract us from our true calling as human beings, as God's subjects: meditation and prayers and bowing before the Almighty. *Fitna*, on the other hand, is the anti-divine, the anti-social, that which ruptures the order and peace of society. Mernissi (1987) claims that Islam views women as the embodiment of destruction and disorder: 'The woman is *fitna*, the epitome of the uncontrollable, a living representative of the dangers of sexuality and its rampant disruptive potential' (p. 44).

Evoking the disruptive powers of *fitna*, Siddiqui (1999, June) takes umbrage at the 'psychologically unstable and neurotic women on the payroll of Western NGOs in the service of spreading shamelessness in traditional cultures' (p. 48). He considers the propagation of notions like 'women's rights' to be nothing less than a planned disruption in the traditional structures of family. 'Alas,' he sighs, 'floodgates should have been drawn against this *fitna* in the beginning' (p. 48). In Urdu literature, however, the beloved is

ironically mentioned as a *fitna*—a temptress *par excellence*, who by
definition leads the believer, the righteous man, astray.[26] In Arabic,
Persian, and Urdu poetry *fitna* has been used to connote the
ultimate chaos, that of the Day of Judgment. In a couplet, Ghalib,
considered to be the most significant Urdu poet of the nineteenth
century, uses it thus:

> *Jub tuk kay naa daikha thaa qad-e-yaar kaa aalam*
> *Mein mu'atqad-e-fitna-e-mahshar naa hoo'aa thaa*

> Until the moment that I was enchanted by the graces of my beloved,
> I really hadn't known the *fitna* that would unleash on the Day of
> Judgment.[27]

Siddiqui's (June 1999) fears, are borne out by Mernissi's (1987)
observation that, the fear of women's self-determination is basic to
the Muslim order and is closely linked to fear of *fitna*. The idea
being that if 'women are not constrained, then men are faced with
an irresistible sexual attraction that inevitably leads to *fitna* and
chaos by driving them to illicit copulation'. (pp. 53–54) Muslim
social structure, then, can be seen as a defence against the disorder
in social life that can be unleashed by the *fitna* of which the
women's attributes are viewed as capable. So, it probably goes
without saying that honour is *afitnatic*.

The magic world, according to Kramer (1997), is saturated with
a vital force or energy in various cultures conceptualized as *mana*,
karma, or *chi*. Fitna, I argue, is of the same chthonic centre where
the *élan vital* of life resides. If *mana*, *karma*, and *chi* are about peace
and quiet, *fitna* is about unrest and chaos. Each being the antithesis
of the other, the one is not possible without the other. The eternal
process of resolution in their tension is the fundamental organic
process of life, their movement towards a synthesis is the march of
time.

GHAIRAT AUR TAANA (HONOUR AND SOCIAL RIDICULE)

In order to understand the killing of women by men of their family to address the breach of honour, it is important to look into the communicative milieu of the group and the role that the man's cohort plays. In Pakistan, which is a collective society where honour is important, a man is supposed to be the guardian and the arbiter of his own honour. He is solely responsible for protecting it. To feel dishonoured and to avenge it lies in the domain of the magical and the mythical. The rationalized laws of the perspectival world have no bearing on it since the code of honour derives from an inherited sacred quality of the man and not from secular ethical or juridical provisions. The individual has to face up to it with his primal resources. On the other hand, in the mental realm, one sues for libel. And, to seek recompense from law, according to Pitt-Rivers (1970), 'places your honour in jeopardy, a jeopardy from which the satisfaction of legal compensation at the hands of secular authority hardly redeems it (p. 30).

However, in the magical and the mythical worlds the opinions of the society are critical. Although honour is perceived individually (i.e., privately), the damage to honour relates to the range of public that comes to know about it. In Pitt-Rivers' (1970) view, public opinion is like 'the court of reputation' against whose judgment there is no redress; public ridicule kills. In this section I explore how a man is pressured through ridicule to act according to the unwritten but well understood code of honour. After all, his honour partakes of the honour of the whole community. His 'cowardice' will be a blot on the honour of all.

During his interview about his concept of honour and the resort to killing by men, Bakram (personal communication, 9 July 2002) dwelt upon the abstract nature of honour. When I asked him if honour is the same for men and women, he said:

> Honour is not something that is sold, that can be bargained over. It resides in the soul. Depending on the culture, people either have it or

they don't. It is not something material that can be measured in ounces and grams.

At this stage, my friend, who had arranged the interview, interrupted our exchange with a copy of *Time* magazine, opened at a full-page photograph of US President George W. Bush with one of his adult daughters near a lake. Probably an election promotional shot, it represented familial bliss in a rustic setting if seen from the modern Western perspective. Holding some fishing equipment, Bush was engrossed in explaining some finer points about fishing. The reason my friend presented the photograph for our scrutiny was the attire of the president's daughter. He was in Abercrombie roughs and she was wearing cut-offs. For members of a society where the veil is *de rigueur*, such attire on a woman—especially in the presence of her father—is not considered honourable.

My friend: Look at these clothes in which his daughter is going fishing with Bush. Do you think he is *bay ghairat* (without honour)?

Bakram: (Obviously evading the bait) Whatever it may be but the world pays respect to Bush.

Jafri: But Bush says that he is bombing Afghanistan because the American sense of *ghairat* (honour) has been challenged. How is this sense of honour different from the sense of honour for which one kills one's own sister or daughter? Is honour different for people in different places? Why is the son of Adam behaving differently in different places?

Bakram: Some of Adam's children have also opted to be monkeys and bears and dogs. God himself punished some nations by willing them to be monkeys. (Bakram was getting riled now. The restraint he had shown until now about expressing political opinion started to crack). Now with a raised voice, he continued: They can bomb Afghanistan all they want but they cannot succeed.

Jafri: I really was not talking about politics. Do you think that the notion of honour was different in the time of Jesus or in the time of Mohammad (PBUH) from what it is now in our society?

Bakram: (Doesn't address the question) Taliban had control over their domain. They were simple people. Their ministers had simple lunch with light yogurt, treated people well, demonstrated true Islam.

Jafri: We were actually talking about the difference, qualitative difference, between the act of the husband who kills his wife out of sudden provocation and that of the male members who kill their women in cold blood in order to restore their honour. These men don't hide and hire lawyers like they do in the West. Rather, they walk with their head up in their neighbourhood. What is that?

Bakram: Islam says stone the fornicator. That is only way you can retain your honour.

Jafri: Does one kill because of the pressure from tradition?

Bakram: Yes, out of compulsion. What would people say when I walk in the neighbourhood? Do you want me to respond from the Islamic perspective?

Jafri: No, I am not talking about Islam necessarily. All I want to understand is, Why do men kill women they love?

Bakram: Because people give them *taanaa* (taunt, reproach, jeer, sarcasm, etc.) that this is what the woman of your house did. When the woman is killed at least the *taanaa zani* (the subtle ways that in a circumstance like this taunting permeates the neighbourhood discourse) stops.

Jafri: Can we become *ghairat mand* (honourable)? Since you say that as a nation we have become *bay ghairat* (without honour; as is probably clear, the two, *bay ghairat* and *ghairat mand* are opposites.), can I ask you if we can become—as individuals—*ghairat mand*?

Bakram: Of course you can. The short cut is repentance and accepting Islam.

Taanaa is a much more eloquent word in original Arabic than the various English meanings would express. In the Caravan Dictionary alone (Feroze, 2001), seven different entries exist for it from the delivery of *taanaa* to who can deliver it and who can be the recipient of it. The dictionary does not mention it but Shakespeare's 'slings and arrows' comes closest to the spirit of *taanaa.* (Except in the bard's case, slings flew from the saddle-strap of circumstance. *Taanaa zani* is analogous to the 'buttons' close relatives and friends push in order to 'drive us up the wall.') In the local communicative milieu *taanaa* expresses scorn with sarcasm indirectly with subtle use of innuendo, allusion, and metaphor. Unlike a curse, abuse, profanity or other forms of put-downs, which are direct and blunt, *taanaa* is oblique, sometimes shrouded in peripheral narratives, presented as fables, and tinctured with sneers and smiles. In collective societies, because of being mentioned repeatedly for a variety of purposes, these narratives are familiar to the ingroup with the complexity and allusive complicity of all their possible meanings. The words and how they are uttered are significant in such a sensitive situation because, as Pitt-Rivers (1970) puts it, they are both 'expressions of attitude, which claim, accord or deny honour. Honour, however, is only irrevocably committed by attitudes expressed in the presence of witnesses, the representatives of public opinion'. (p. 27) Indeed, in societies such as these there are people who are considered particularly adept at delivering *taanaa*. As the *taanaas* are delivered, the pressure builds up on the target-individual and (s)he is closely monitored for reaction.

Shah (1998, November 19) agrees that the social pressure on the individual from within the ingroup is the driving force for the act of killing itself:

> The triggering point of a man's passionate urge to kill would just be a comment he would hear in the marketplace. This is called a *tano*[28]—a Sindhi word for insinuation and insult mixed together. It renders him socially impotent. The *tano* would be very subtle but for any *mard* (man) it would be enough to declare war on culprits. Violence to retrieve this honour may be a means through which the illusion of wholeness is reasserted.

What Shah calls 'illusion to wholeness' is the hallmark of the magic or the mythic world. Borrowing from Sorokin, Geertz (1973) calls this aspect of culture the 'causal-functional integration.' This contrasts with Geertz's 'logico-meaningful integration.' The two aspects correspond with what Gebser (1985) characterized as the aperspectival/magic and the perspectival/mental structures of consciousness. Geertz (1973) elucidates:

> By logico-meaningful integration, characteristic of the social system, is meant the sort of integration one finds in a Bach fugue, in a Catholic dogma, or in the general theory of relativity; it is a unity of style, of logical implication, of meaning and value. By causal-functional integration characteristic of the social system, is meant the kind of integration one finds in an organism, where all the parts are united in a single causal web; each part is an element a reverberating causal ring that 'keeps the system going.' (p. 145)

Clearly, in the magic and mythic worlds, in the world of causal-functional integration, messages are not crafted, informed by a logical sequence, but are reflexes that are inbuilt in the system that are communicated automatically. Responses to communicative actions are programmed in the system through an organic co-dependence and cohabitation and do not need to be rationalized. Communication is guileless and innocent of the consideration of consequences. Indeed, it is impervious to possible ramifications brought on by the law of the times.

SUMMARY

In this chapter I looked into certain representative contemporary discourses in Pakistan and how certain concepts related to honour killing are articulated in order to set the standards of conduct for women in society. For this, I parsed certain concepts like the veil, pollution, space, honour killing as expiation, the dialectic of order and chaos, and the idea of public ridicule and insult as a spur to address the perceived loss of honour. The concept of honour is a mythic one. It belongs to a world where the good and the evil are known to all, and the members of the community are expected to abide by it—come what may. In mythical societies, the transactions of honour in the rituals of daily existence are the means by which the roles of individuals in the social organization are congealed; individuals are expected by other members of the culture to take these social roles seriously.

The next chapter deals with the role of honour in individualistic and collectivistic societies. First, I look at the discourses generated from the Pakistani judiciary. This will include judgments in specific cases of honour killing that should be viewed as messages sent to the citizens about the modes of acceptable behaviour, and to the world community about what kind of a society Pakistan views itself to be. Similarly, the statements of the senators during the senate debate on honour killing are important texts to understand the viewpoint of the people's representatives. The defeat of the motion to condemn honour killing by a margin of 96–4 was also a message, albeit a chilling one, an indicator of the ethical direction of the country. Finally, borrowing from feminist literature the terms 'agency' and 'interruption,' I discuss the ways these empowering concepts are being played out by the various strands of feminism in Pakistan.

NOTES

1. Non Governmental Organizations (NGOs), most often based in technologically advanced Western countries, make structural contributions in countries that range from accelerated decay and chaos to having some development activities. The World Bank defines NGOs as 'private organizations that pursue activities to relieve suffering, promote the interests of the poor, protect the environment, provide basic social services, or undertake community development' (Operational Directive 14.70). In wider usage, the term NGO may be applied to any non-profit organization independent from government. NGOs are typically value-based organizations that depend, in whole or in part, on charitable donations and voluntary service. Although the NGO sector has become increasingly corporate-like during the past two decades, principles of altruism and voluntarism remain key defining characteristics.

2. *Qari* refers to someone who recites the Quran. Reciting of the Quran in all its lilting melody is an entrenched Islamic tradition. In *madrasahs* (religious schools) boys (usually) are taught to read Arabic and recite the verses from the Quran from an early age. It is not uncommon for a boy to know the full text of the Quran by heart by the time he is eight years old. Usually, those who excel at reciting from memory and doing it well are given the title *Qari*.

3. Formerly known as Lyallpur (named in memory of Lord Lyall—echoes of the Raj), Faisalabad (renamed in memory of King Faisal of Saudi Arabia—echoes of Pakistan's new economic masters) is a major industrial town in Pakistan. In order to express their strong identity with their culture, people in the subcontinent, especially poets and orators, often use the name of their village/town with their name. This bespeaks the strong identity that people have with their environs in the magic and mythic realms (See Gebser, 1985; Kramer, 1997). Clearly, for those in the social limelight, this serves a political purpose too.

4. Historically *madrasahs* were—and some still are—peaceful centres for theological and philosophical learning in Islamic societies. According to Stern (2000), 'In the 1980s, Pakistani dictator, General Ziaul Haq promoted the *madrasahs* as a way to garner the religious support for his rule and to recruit troops for the anti-Soviet war in Afghanistan ... *madrasahs* have become a supply line for jihad' (p. 117).

5. The primary sources of law in Pakistan are the Holy Quran and *Ahadith* (plural of *hadith*). The Quran consists of what are considered to be divine revelations and is divided into chapters and verses. It is considered the absolute word of God by Muslims. If the divine revelations do not cover the fact of a certain case than the dicta of the Holy Prophet, to whom cases used to be brought for decision, are treated as supplementary to the Divine Ordinance. These dicta, compiled during the early days of Islam by members of the Prophet's close circle, are called *Ahadith*. (Among others see Patel, 1991.) In Guillame's (1966) view, 'The *hadith* literature...provides us with apostolic precept and example covering the whole duty of man; it is the basis of that developed system of law, theology, and custom which is Islam' (p. 5). According to Walther (1993), 'From the eighth century on, these *Hadiths*, which the orientalists call prophetic "traditions" were recorded in great compendia. Six of these compendia became canonical, particularly those of Bukhari (d. 870) and of Muslim (d. 875)' (p. 48). These are important for Islamic societies as Prophet Muhammad's (PBUH) life is considered a model of how a Muslim should deal with and find solutions to their daily problems.

6. There is much debate about the veil, its literal and metaphorical importance, and its implementation in the context of Islamic teachings (see Mernissi, 1987). The idea was converted into a slogan and disingenuously used to push an ultra conservative agenda in Pakistan by the dictator Ziaul Haq during 1977–85.

7. Borrowing from Hall, Mernissi (1987) spotlights an extremely interesting and relevant point: 'The notion of trespassing is related not so much to physical boundaries as to the identity of the person performing the act. A friend, for example, never trespasses, while a foe always does' (p. 143). In certain Moroccan folklore (as in several others) women are considered

depositories of devilish forces, hence foes to men who are 'regular' human beings.

8. *Ash-Shaitan* (called Lucifer in the Bible) is supposed to lead God's creation, humanity, astray.

9. Women's increasing participation in Pakistani national life can be gauged from their recent triumph in electoral politics. According to Cowasjee (9 March 2003), after the October 2002 elections, there are 212 women legislators in the four provincial assemblies and 17 senators in the national senate.

10. For *purdah,* Feroze (2001) includes 'a curtain,' 'a screen,' 'secrecy,' 'privacy,' 'modesty,' and 'lid (of the eye)' as definitions.

11. Interestingly, 'prophet' is called *paighaam-bar* in Farsi and Urdu. The Urdu equivalent connotes not 'someone who prophesies' or 'visionary' as in English, but someone who is the 'carrier of the message.' In Arabic, the language of the Quran, the word is *nabi* a derivative of the Hebrew *navi,* meaning "spokesman" (Stillman, personal communication, 27 February 2003). In this case, the privileged and the pious one whom God chose and trusts to diffuse His message among the people.

12. *Paleed* is translated as 'polluted' (Feroze, 2001). Interestingly, in their respective languages, both words are loaded with mythic and religious significance of negativity. According to Young (1992), 'The word of pollution in every culture means the bad breath of divinity, and infectious, contagious affliction that calls for the quarantine and cleansing (Greek *katharsis*) of every thing and person who has been exposed to it' (p. 232).

13. 'Pollution' comes from the Latin *polluere* meaning 'defile,' and *pollere,* meaning to be 'powerful' (p. 232, Young 1992).

14. Triandis (1985) says, 'Ingroups are groups of individuals about whose welfare a person is concerned, with whom that person is willing to cooperate without demanding equitable returns, and separation from whom leads to anxiety. Outgroups are groups with which one has something to divide, perhaps unequally, or are harmful in some way; groups that disagree on valued attributes; or groups with which one is in conflict" (p. 9). Triandis (1985) adds: "Even a member of a kin group can become an outgroup member if there are insults, improper behaviour, or conflict over property. For example, in many collectivistic cultures, 'crimes of honour' involve a father or brother killing their daughter or sister who has broken an important taboo, such as having premarital sexual relations. Among collectivists, who value homogeneity, when a relationship with another group is characterized by long time conflict, ethnic cleansing can be seen as a 'natural' consequence" (p. 10). This discussion increases in relevance as we get into the discussion about individualist and collectivist cultures.

15. He is talking about Habib Rehman, the driver/gunman who killed Samia in the office of the lawyer, Jilani.

16. Laws and rules about the women's veil go back more than 4,000 years. According to Lerner (1986), the idea of the veil evolved from the need to distinguish between respectable and disrespectable women. Women were considered respectable if they sexually served and were under the protection of one man; these women were veiled. Those women not under one man's protection and sexual control were designated as 'public women' and were supposed to be unveiled. Lerner (1986) quotes Middle Assyrian Law #40: 'Neither [wives] of [seignors] nor [widows] nor [Assyrian women] who go out on the street may have their heads uncovered. The daughters of a seignior ... whether it is a shawl or a robe or [a mantle], must veil themselves. A concubine who goes out on the street with her mistress must veil herself. A sacred prostitute whom a man married must veil herself on the street, but one whom a man did not marry must have her head uncovered on the street; she must not veil herself. A harlot must not veil herself; her head must be uncovered' (p. 134).

17. Interestingly, Pickthall (1996/30) translates *libaas* as 'raiment.' As equal partners, men and women, then, are each other's ornaments, as raiments apart from enhancing physical beauty protect by acting as a shield against the elements. Shakespeare's (1600) lines in Sonnet xxii about 'raiment' are noteworthy in this context too: 'For all that beauty that doth cover thee / Is but the seemly raiment of my heart / Which in thy breast doth live, as in me' (p. 13).

18. Pilgrimage to Mecca is one of the tenets of Islam. He who accomplishes it is called *haji*.

19. To be described as 'Indian' in Pakistan (or vice versa) evokes high degrees of suspicion and animosity. Weaver's (1953) distinction of devil terms and god terms is relevant in this situation. For Pakistanis to watch movies, particularly those 'too Indian,' is 'unpatriotic and dishonourable,' and therefore, doubly reprehensible.

20. Mentioning the act of cutting the offensive woman to pieces and betrothing her in the same furious fit is revealing of several aspects of how women are conceptualized by the extreme religious fringe elements of the culture. First, the sexual act is described as being performed on (rather than 'with') a woman, and that the act is essentially a holy duty (to proliferate the race) performed reluctantly and with disdain. Second, equating the act of sex with 'cutting her to bits,' rather clearly reveals anger and hostility toward women. Third, and perhaps most importantly, his statement belies the pity and disgust that he feels for such 'polluted' women. In class terms, this is the equivalent of *noblesse oblige* or, to borrow from Rudyard Kipling, 'white man's burden.'

21. (Feroze, 2001) translates *bay purdigi* as 'immodesty,' 'shamelessness,' 'indecency,' 'openness,' but metaphorically it points towards a certain wanton nonchalance about personal conduct. Literally, *bay purdigi* means

not being properly veiled. In certain societies for women not to be veiled is profane and thus sneered at.

22. I have done a literal translation in order to express the rhetorical effect of words in the Urdu language on the audience. Faisalabadi, in a breathtaking hyperbole, equates the Quran with the veil and shame by having Jesus raise the sanctity of the veil and shame equal to that of the Quran.

23. According to Gebser (1985), 'The very original meaning of the word "religion" (from *relegere*) indicates 'careful observance' and is the opposite of 'negligence' (from *neglegare*), 'careless non-observance' (p. 63).

24. The Caravan Urdu-English dictionary (2001) translates *fitna* variously as 'sedition,' 'revolt,' 'riot,' 'intrigue,' 'wickedness,' 'mischief,' 'trouble,' and, interestingly, 'playful sweetheart.' None of these translations, nor a combination of them, quite encompasses the Biblical destructive powers of *fitna*. According to Mernissi (1987) '*fitna* also means 'beautiful woman'—the connotation of a *femme fatale* who makes men lose their self-control' (p. 31). The Arabic-English dictionary (Baolbaki, 1995) translates *fitna* as 'enchant,' 'seduce,' 'tempt,' 'magic,' 'sedition,' 'disorder,' 'tumult.' *Fitna*, according to Lane (1956) causes 'a man to enter into fire' (app. by way of trial or probation), and (in like manner) in a state of punishment or affliction (p. 2334)'.

25. *Sirat ul mustaqeem* (the righteous path) is a recurrent theme of the Quran. Here I have cited only the first verse.

26. The closest term for the woman as *fitna* in the Western lexicon that I found was *femme fatale*. Webster's New Collegiate Dictionary (1979) defines it as 'disastrous woman,' 'a seductive woman who lures men into compromising situations,' 'a woman who attracts men by an aura of charm and mystery' (p. 418).

27. Ghalib is also the most famous poet of the Urdu language and has been translated worldwide. With this couplet, however, by translating him, I take the liberty of using my lifelong crossings of the borders between Urdu and English.

28. Sindh is the original eponymous word for Indus (the land where the Indus, the river originally called *Sindh*, flows). Sindhi is the language spoken in the Sindh province. Like Urdu, Sindhi borrows freely from Arabic. *Tano*, as seems obvious, is the Sindhi derivative of *taanaa*.

5

Discourses of Power

In the previous chapter I discussed how some messages are formulated, sent, and perceived in Pakistani society by the various discourse communities. Because language is the basic mediating tool between culture and community, the style and substance of these linguistic messages provide useful material to understand the development of certain attitudes in the community. Some of these statements were not specifically about honour killing but sought to instruct their male audience members about the nature of honour and the female members about acceptable conduct in society. To support their arguments, the religious preachers presented examples from the sacred texts; some, such as the mullah I interviewed, suggested supra-religious means in order to keep the structures of the society intact. I also discussed how important it is in Pakistan for individuals to be concerned about the opinions of fellow members of the community. In collectivist societies, such as Pakistan, the loss of honour of an individual is perceived to be the loss of honour of the community. Sometimes because of the use of ridicule and innuendo (*taanaa*) the individual is left with 'no choice' except to do whatever it takes to restore the community honour. Honour killing is one such extreme measure.

In the beginning of this study, I had posited that although honour killing is an ancient practice, the sudden discussion around the phenomenon is a result of the resurgence of the mythic structures of consciousness in the face of the dominant mental/rational consciousness structures. In this chapter I shall look at the texts of the various discourse communities—the senate, the feminists, the activists, and other leaders of public opinion—where the conflicting nature of the two modes of consciousness come to the fore. Later in the chapter, borrowing from literature on feminism, I explore the ideas of 'agency' and 'interruption' as they relate to women and power.

INDIVIDUALISTIC AND COLLECTIVISTIC CULTURES

The tension between the rights of the individual in the society and those of the society over the individual are at the heart of the ongoing discussion about honour killing. To conflate, the individual, a woman, acts out of personal passion, a psychological impulse, biological need, and so on; the family perceives it to be a breach of the honour, and the male members of the family kill the woman.[1] When the conflict between the individual and the collective develops in such a fundamental way, the issue of whose rights can have ascendancy comes to the fore. One has to bear in mind that 'individualistic' and 'collectivistic' are binary theoretical abstracts and not 'total' ways in which any society functions. Societies only *tend* to be either collectivistic or individualistic.

According to Gebser (1985), collectivism and individualism are also the hallmarks of magic/mythic (pre-rational/irrational) and mental (rational) structures of consciousness, respectively. The archaic[2] structure of which the magic and the mythic partake as a nascent form is a time when the soul of man is dormant and a complete non-differentiation exists between man and the universe. The individual, at one with the surrounding universe, is completely subsumed under the collective. Over a period of time, as the magic and the mythic realms have become devitalized and as the mental has gained strength, so have collective cultures yielded to individualistic ways of structuring life. According to Gebser (1985), 'The contemporary "primitives" no longer live in the archaic, but in a more or less deficient magic structure'. (p. 44) Similarly, I argue, societies such as Pakistan function in deficient mythic structures as they grapple with the demands of the modern, the mental, and the increasing social and personal dissociation and atomism. Collectivistic societies thrive in the mythic when nature and culture are more or less aligned. On the other hand, according to Kramer (2001), 'When or wherever modernity is manifested ...

there is a separation between culture and nature'. (p. 27) Since the origins of various understandings—and thus social behaviour like honour killing—are rooted in the structures of awareness, it is important to explore through the various discourses how the mythic and the mental, the traditional and the modern, and the collectivist and the individualist interface in Pakistan.

From the statistical analysis on Mead's (1967) data examining cooperation and competition among primitive people, Triandis (1988) discovered that while individualistic cultures emphasized self-interest, the collectivistic cultures held the good of the ingroup central to their identity. He concluded that no society is purely individualistic or collectivistic but situation-specific. However, in his view, the individualistic-collectivistic binary is a useful template that can be utilized to identify motivations and tendencies in a culture. In Hofstede's (2001) view, the most pertinent distinction between the individualistic and the collectivistic cultures that sociology can offer is the one by Tonnies (1963, first published 1887) between *Gemeinschaft* (low individualism) and *Gesellschaft* (high individualism). In certain societies, the self is submerged and totally identified with the culture and in some the individuals have yielded completely to the alienating, the centrifugal tendencies. For example, Hsu (1971) tells us that the Chinese tradition is bereft of the Western concept of personality as distinct from its culture. The Chinese word for man (*ren*) includes the person's intimate cultural identity and this accounts for the meaningfulness of the individual's life. My own family members in Pakistan still identify themselves with the village where their ancestors lived several generations ago.[3] In collectivistic societies, for rituals such as arrangement of marriages, such groundings are of paramount importance. The last name of the orator Qari Abdul Hafeez Faisalabadi[4] (see Chapter V), also points toward the same tendency. This is in stark contrast to the hyper-modernist cultures where the individual follows the intensely personal 'self actualizing'[5] track.

Kramer (1997) calls this tendency to look at such phenomena in binaries, to categorize human societies in individualistic and collectivistic as 'Aristotelian, two-valued logic which defines a world with no middle, no maybe' (p. 34). Human societies are not, indeed cannot be, purely individualistic or collectivistic, but rather function on the spectrum that lies between the two idealized extremes. Only archaic societies, functioning in what Gebser (1985) called the magic structures of consciousness, could have had a strong enough cohesion among their members to be called exclusively 'collective.' Similarly, despite the condition of hyper-modernity in certain societies, there are no purely 'individualistic' cultures.

In cultures that tend toward the collective form of psychological bonding, identification among the members of the group is intense. Thus these cultures are the epitome of the fraternal. On the other hand, in the hypothetically complete 'individualistic' culture, the idea of individual freedom and liberty will be so foundational that, to borrow from John Donne, all individuals would be completely sovereign islands, bereft of organic connects with each other, with only legal responsibilities towards the state and each other as sovereign individuals. In Kramer's (1997) words, 'Magic identity is collectivistic to the extreme' (p. xiii). On the other hand Kramer states that in hyper-modernity, an individual becomes his/her own clan. The accrual of dimensions from here increases awareness and dissociation. Progress triggers the process of fragmentation and alienation and the shift towards perspectival consciousness. An individual's rights and liberty also are modern concepts contributing to the tension between the human desire for liberty and need for fraternity. In Paz's (1991) view, 'The Modern Age has exalted individualism and has been, therefore, the period of the scattering and isolation of personal awareness' (pp. 69–70). This is the direction away from collective responsibility toward each other and veers in the direction of solipsism, personal indulgence, and the angst that are concomitants of modernity and individualism. Baudelaire even puts a moral judgment on the phenomenon, 'But the universal ruin (or universal progress: the name matters little to me) will manifest itself not in political institutions, but instead in the debasement of our souls' (p. 70; quoted in Paz, 1991). What Gebser (1985) calls the unperspectival consciousness or the magic world, Freud (1950) brands as animism. 'Animism,' Freud (1950) explains, 'does not merely give an explanation of a particular phenomenon, but allows us to grasp the whole universe as a single unity from a single point of view' (p. 97).

Ting-Toomey (1994) also points out that cross cultural studies (Hofstede, 1980, 1991; Hui & Triandis, 1986; Schwartz & Bilsky, 1990; Triandis, Brislin, & Hui, 1988; Wheeler, Reis, & Bond, 1989) have provided ample theoretical and empirical evidence that numerous cultures function with the value orientation of individualism and collectivism. Ting-Toomey (1994) fails to point out that for cultures to be individualistic and collectivistic is not a *value*; rather it is a way of being prior to judgment. This orientation influences the process and outcomes of different types of conflicts between the individual and the collective. According to Ting-Toomey (1994):

> Basically, *individualism* refers to the broad value tendencies of a culture to emphasize the importance of individual identity over group rights, individual rights over group rights, and individual needs over group needs. In contrast, *collectivism* refers to the broad value tendencies of a culture to emphasize the importance of the 'we' identity over the 'I' identity, group obligations over individual rights, and ingroup-oriented needs over individual wants and desires. (p. 360-361)

Niazi (7 May 1999) calls the controversy about honour killing 'a dilemma within our social fabric which we have dimly realized.' I understand this dilemma to be the result of the Gebserian perspectival/mental meeting the unperspectival/magic/mythic structures of consciousness in the Pakistani society. What Niazi (7 May 1999) calls 'tribal ethos' is nothing but the mythical consciousness, and the 'settled way of life' the perspectival/mental/rational/modern. It is important to note that the use of the term 'settled way of life' here should not be taken literally to mean the lack of physical mobility of individuals. As discussed earlier, that is a characteristic of the mythical structure of consciousness. Metaphorically, 'settled way of life' stands for the society whose social and legal structures are rational, well considered, and well-established; in a word 'settled.' This is the hallmark of the perspectival where individuals live under a social contract with the state with clearly itemized rights and responsibilities. On the other hand, in the mythic (the 'tribal') where the rights of the collective and tradition hold sway, rights and duties of the individual are to be understood within the largely unwritten code of the clan. One lives for the sacred interests and honour of the clan and not to uphold the secular laws of the land. Niazi's (7 May 1999) understanding of 'tribal' and 'settled' is not removed from what communication scholars understand as 'collective' and 'individualistic':

> The settled way of life is based on the perception that, while common interests have to be taken into account, the greatest good is individual satisfaction ... therefore individual rights are the basic building blocks of social life and the sanctity of life is an axiomatic goal. On the other hand, the tribal way of life postulates the role of the individual as merely a component of a larger unit with well-defined responsibilities and functions. The corollaries are that individual rights are not as important, individual needs are less important than the good of the collective, and life is not as important: it is not so important to avoid death, and it is easier to kill.

It is important to note that it is not only the women who are deemed 'sacrificable' for the sake of the collective harmony, but it seems so because mythical/collectivistic societies tend to be fiercely patriarchal. In order to guard individual and collective honour, a tetchy posture is presented to the outgroup members and not much excuse is needed to take offence. Communication is deliberate and inbuilt hierarchies are respected compared to the modern societies where all adults have equal rights under the law and communication between individuals is generic. Codes of behaviour are woven in the fabric of the context rather than displayed in manuals of law. Men of honour settle their differences by themselves. They scorn the help of lawyers. The mythic (what Niazi calls 'tribal') world is not legalistic. Nuanced gestures and expressions of mutual respect characterize interactions because people are conscious that rude behaviour or perceived insults can trigger feuds. Since feuds can be bloody and long-lasting, they usually do not break out over trifles but over the proverbial *zan, zar, zameen* (women, gold, land).[6] Life is not considered too important in an ethos bristling with such machismo. Money is *marad kay haath kaa may'l* (dirt on a man's palm). Death is a shrug. But honour is important. It is because of honour that even in minor conflicts between people of the mythic world, face-saving is of utmost importance. And, although women are respected as mothers and as vital connections in communication with other kinship groups or as a means of nurturing relations within the group, they can be disposed of if they are perceived to deviate from the automatically understood strict social codes.

SAMIA'S KILLING AND THE INDIVIDUALISM-COLLECTIVISM PARADIGM

Usually, in collectivistic societies actions taken by individuals that can be viewed by the group as egotistical, narcissistic, and a transgression of the prescribed bounds of behaviour in the specific cultural setting can trigger a response by other group members. On the other hand, actions taken by the individual to affirm group values are lauded by the members of the group. For example, though Samia Sarwar's killing was condemned as a savage measure by human rights and other groups, obliquely, she was perceived to have brought it on herself by other powerful discourse communities.

THE PAKISTAN SENATE

During the discussion in the senate about the resolution to condemn Samia's murder, Senator Bilour, after establishing his own fondness and familiarity with Samia since she was a little girl, and grief over her death, underscores Sarwar's (Samia's father) tragic loss and suffering: 'He lost his driver, his daughter, and faces charges of murder.' Bilour lays the most emphasis on Sarwar's piety, moral high standing, and service to the group. As Bilour sees it, he underscores Sarwar's role as an upright member of his community: 'He is not ignorant; he is an educated man, he has an MA in English; he is the president of the Chamber of Commerce; he has been a member of foreign delegations with Nawaz Sharif, Farooq

Leghari, and Benazir Bhutto.[7] He was not philandering, sir! What sin did he commit? He had gone for *haj*[8] and had taken his wife with him to do God's bidding.' He then contrasts such group-conforming behaviours with Samia's group-defying, self-serving, and egotistical indulgence:

> What does she do when the parents are at *haj*? She elopes to Lahore.[9] And what, may I ask in my humble way, was a married woman, a mother of two doing meeting with an outside man for several hours at the women's shelter? Sir, for God's sake, try to understand: the father is at *haj*, the mother is at *haj*, what kind of human behaviour is this? What kind of human rights are these? What kind of *sharafat*[10] is this? In reality, we should talk about the murder of Habib ur Rehman. Who did that? Who ordered that? (Verbatim Record of the Proceedings of the Senate, 10 May 1999, 96th session, p. 33)

It is important to note that one of the characteristics of an individualistic/ modern/legalistic society is the freedom of association for adults. Thus marriage and divorce in such cultures are fundamentally personal affairs in which family and friends may or may not have much interest. In collectivistic cultures, marriages are arrangements between families and divorces can potentially trigger generational feuds. For the sake of their family honour, Samia's parents were resisting the idea of divorce. Samia had been separated from her allegedly abusive husband for a couple of years and had been desperately trying to get a divorce at the time of the incident. However, she deviated from her community's traditional standards of conduct by associating with another man. Even the highest law-enacting body of the country could not endorse such encroachment of the modern on the mythical, or such individual disregard for the collective.

On the other hand, Bilour evoked sympathy for Habib ur Rehman, the Sarwar family driver/gunman, who actually killed Samia. The senate, in Bilour's view, should have really addressed the more important issue: that is the murder of Habib ur Rehman who gave his life for the honour of his masters (Samia's parents) and the community. The implication was that Rehman's was an unpleasant duty, but for the sake of the community's honour he fulfilled his duty heroically and paid the ultimate price.

Concern for Habib ur Rehman was also voiced by Senator Haji Abdul Rehman who started by asking the Chair of the Senate about the legitimacy of women's shelters: 'How can a *bachi*,[11] who is betrothed, be kept in some institution? By what law? What religion? What were the forces that facilitated this kidnapping? Who orchestrated these *murders*?'

By pluralizing 'murder,' Senator Rehman brings the two murders—one of a legally innocent woman, the other of someone who committed a murder a few minutes before—on the same moral and legal planes, the doings of the same demonic forces. This sets the stage for taking the spotlight from Samia's to Habib ur Rehman's killing: 'Sir, you need to think about who is the real murderer, in whose house the murder took place. Who orchestrated the kidnapping? And who killed the driver? That is the question.' And then, he uses a devil term (Weaver, 1953): 'That place [the women's shelter] is a den of prostitution.' For the four senators who voted to pass the resolution condemning the so-called honour killing, he said: 'Do they come to the Senate to protect such prostitution dens?' Nobody—certainly no senator in the Islamic Republic of Pakistan—can afford to be viewed as a protector of prostitution dens! The women's rights lawyers, representing in this case the modern, the perspectival, and the individual's rights are thus accused of running prostitution dens if they fight for the rights of individual women and defy the community's traditions. By labelling Samia's move to the women's shelter as a 'kidnapping to a prostitution den' Senator Rehman (no relation of Habib ur Rehman) underscores the community's debt to Habib ur Rehman who, by killing Samia, salvaged its honour. The senators' rhetoric has clear implications: Sad as Samia's killing was, she asked for it; now, we need to investigate those who are polluting our culture with imported notions of human rights and the like. Additionally, it is implied that these importers of pollution should be tried for running prostitution dens and for murder.

PUBLIC OPINION

Ahmed (7 September 1999) addresses the impasse between the individual, women in the case of honour killing, and the collective:

> Most of our society is under siege of our archaic morality rules that are reinforced with the religious orthodoxy and tribal ethos[12] . . . betraying such traditions is tantamount to declaring war on one's own family, society, and the tribe that reacts to disloyalty violently under the same warfare rules required to preserve the honour of religious beliefs or protect the possession of property.

As this naturalizing rhetoric makes clear, Ahmed (7 September 1999) plainly exists in a deficient mythic structure of consciousness and presents a utopian version of his society in which the sense of identity of the individuals is complete with the universe—family, society, religion, property, etc.—around it.

What Ahmed (7 September 1999) calls the 'siege of our archaic morality' echoes Kramer's (1997) articulation of the magic world that is marked by idolic communication and where identity is collectivistic in the extreme. Reflex to violence by the male member of the culture is visceral and not a considered decision. The world in the magic consciousness, in Kramer's (1997) words, is '...finished and perfect. In such a world, ideas like improvement, development, progress, and correction are profane if even thinkable' (p. xiv). Honour killing, being different from passion killing, is a cold and calculated murder in the service of preserving a myth of the culture. In the mythic world, too, the idea of women's rights is outside the purview of prescribed family roles and social positions, representing a form of profanity, because such rights are an attempt at 'improvement,' etc. Such ideas are foreign (literally, too) to them, are considered contaminants, and as such are unsettling and create social dissonance. This can result in quick retaliation. Yousufzai (6 May 1999) is representative of this entrenched position:

> True-blooded *Pakhtuns* would never allow some bodies to dismantle the most revered assets of *Pakhtu* and *Pakhtunwali* in the garb of

feminism and human rights ... nobody should be allowed to tamper
with the *Pakhtun*—Honour and *Ghairat* which are the emblems of the
Pakhtuns code of life—*Pakhtunwali* distinguishing and singularizing
Pakhtun nation among other races ... with their most Westernized
mindset they could not grasp the bare fact that a true-blooded *Pakhtun*
would never compromise when his *nang* (honour, esteem, reputation,
shame, disgrace, etc.) is put at stake.

During some of the interviews conducted, and in certain other
samples of the opinions of the representatives of the various
discourse communities, the idea of Western values and imported
ideologies occurred repeatedly. The two senators, Rehman and
Bilour, made it their central theme during the senate proceedings
about honour killing.

Some of the interviewees, opinion leaders, and social
commentators mentioned it, too. Yousufzai (18 November 1999)
writes: 'This is another case that will enable them [the NGOs and
the human rights activists] to mint money for their[13] Human
Rights Commission of Pakistan from abroad, make more foreign
visits, and humiliate respectable families that refuse to adopt their
degenerate Western ways.' Jan (24 August 1999) asks a rhetorical
question: 'Who is going to set the standard that engagement of
women in extra-marital activities is not immoral, but killing them
is immoral?' And, then he answers it:

> It's an open secret that the donors who fund the women's rights
> activists from abroad are setting and imposing these standards on us
> ... A norm does not need to be invented—it means an enduring
> standard. It is a law of nature, which we ignore at our peril. It is a rule
> of human conduct and a measure of public virtue ... due to the
> imported ideologies, we are fast losing our normative consciousness.

Distancing his culture from the West in fundamental ways,
Siddiqui (June 1999) says:

> If the West, which considers sexual promiscuity to be human instinct,
> is unable to understand the concept of honour and shame as practiced
> in Islamic and Asian societies, we should not be surprised since there

is no word in European languages that can truly compare with *ghairat*. But if the tireless touts of Human Rights demand the death penalty for honour killing we can safely understand that they are inspired by the sick Western ways ... The demand to declare honour killing as murder by the preachers of human rights, at the service of the Western agenda, is not only mischievous but unrealistic.

It is important to note that the above-mentioned opinion makers belong to the perspectival structures of consciousness in which there is a strong presence of the deficient mythical. The simple fact of their writing activity—a defining quality of the rational mode of existence—makes them of the perspectival in Gebserian terms. They are true romantics, too, for they are desperately clinging to notions like the 'blueness' of their blood and comparing their way of life to 'law of nature.' Such notions are informed by the magic and mythic modes of consciousness.

Shamush works for the Amnesty International Office in Karachi, Pakistan. He is the prototype of what certain religious preachers, senators from the tribal areas, and a social commentator called the 'Western-inspired so-called human rights and women's rights activist.' He prides himself on being a modern liberal committed to individual rights and gender equality as spelled out in the Human Rights Charter. I asked him about the relative or universal nature of human rights (Shamush, personal communication, 2 January 2002).

Shamush: Human Rights are universal and they are indivisible. You cannot say that these human rights are for United States of America and these rights should not be adopted in Pakistan.

Jafri: What are those rights? What is the source?

Shamush: Basically, Amnesty is the main document.

Jafri: When was it written?

Shamush: 10 Dec 1948. It was adopted and all those members who are those countries who are the members of the United Nations, they have to adopt the universal declaration of human rights. Even Saudi Arabia is a signatory of that declaration though they have not given rights to the women.

Jafri: Muslim countries signed this document?

Shamush: Yes, they have signed.

Jafri: But I think in Islam you cannot change your religion.

Shamush: I was just pointing out that in Islam you cannot change your religion. But they have signed. They are signatories.

Jafri: But Islam does not allow changing religions?

Shamush: Maybe people should have those rights; particularly those that are considered in conflict with religion. In our tribal areas women are being sold by weight! What religion? What tradition? Unfortunately in Pakistan the laws are in books only. They are not in practice. Laws are not for practice. Not being practiced...you should see the thousands of cases of domestic violence being committed daily ... I will like to say that in spite of the situation, this could be curbed. The situation could be changed. Otherwise this practice is being committed since hundreds of years and still the situation has not changed.

Jafri: OK, this is tribal.

Shamush: This is the tribal gift. Feudal, tribal. And existing laws have gifted us these stupid things. Rather, I think, this is a medieval practice being practiced in the 21st century without any check.

Clearly, Shamush is the archetypal representative of the rational mind. His scorn for the 'medieval' from his rational modern position is clear and understandable. He sees honour killing as an abhorrent practice, a savagery, a remnant of barbaric times. This, in his view, can be eliminated with education and other measures. Shamush embodies the missionary zeal of the progressive rational. His optimism in his claim about the tension between the United Nations charter on human rights, a document representative of the perspectival world, and honour killing, a ritual representing the deeply entrenched attitudes of the mythic world, is also echoed by the president of Amnesty International Pakistan, Dr Habib Soomro. Addressing a press conference launching of AI's report titled 'Honour killing of girls and women in Pakistan,' he said that, once they are accused, women are not even allowed to clear up a possible misunderstanding since tradition dictates only one way to restore male honour: killing the offending women. He echoed Shamush's claim about the ineffectuality of the UN charter: 'Despite having ratified the UN Convention on the Elimination of all forms of

Discrimination Against Women,[14] the government has systematically failed to prevent, investigate, and punish honour killing. We will do what is possible to bring the practice to an end' (AI launches campaign, 1999).

Here, too, we find Pakistan at the interface between the mythic and the mental worlds. On one hand, the United Nations Human Rights Charter is the epitome of a rational/modern document setting up legal rights of human beings across the globe, irrespective of their cultural or religious background. On the other, gender roles and conduct for both men and women are considered timeless and impervious to change in the mythic world. These collectivistic societies are not accepting of rules of conduct prescribed by foreign cultures. If a Muslim steps out of the fold, (s)he is not considered a Muslim anymore but an apostate. In the light of Islamic Law (s)he ought to be killed. Similarly, in the mythic world if a woman transgresses tradition she is no longer a daughter, sister, or a mother, but an adulteress, and honour demands she be killed. This sends a clear message within the group about the way in which such conduct is viewed and hardens the ingroup definition for the outgroups.

Maasoom is a senior officer at the Human Rights Watch office in Karachi. In his view, too, Pakistani society has been stagnating in archaic structures. He considers himself an enlightened modern man. In his view, honour killing occurs because of lack of education. He defended the process of globalization because, in his view, franchises like McDonald's and Kentucky Fried Chicken selling 'Zingers' will be cultural stabilizers.[15] When asked to elaborate, he said, 'Now they are going to change the way we have been looking at things. People representing two different ways of life will start the journey toward an understanding of each other's way of life'. (Maasoom, personal communication, January 3, 2002)

Lack of education, inbuilt structural inequities, and the sway of a tribal ethos, and a complicit or, at best, a passive role of religious institutions in society are the reasons for honour killing that human rights activists generally talked about. Honour killing, in their view, is a manifestation of the discrepancy that is inbuilt in the structural relationships of power, domination, and privilege. In his interview with me, Hassan Taqi of the Human Rights Watch Group (Taqi, personal communication, January 8, 2002) linked honour killing with such national malaises as election fraud or lack of civic amenities. He said the phenomenon of honour killing is not about honour or status, but a part of the large oppressive structure.

FEMINISTS

Having read the views of the senators defending the traditional structures of society and suspicious of imported concepts about individualism and human rights, etc., I sought to interview some of the activist women who represent modernity in Pakistan. One of the most prominent women, equally involved in the peace movement, human rights, and feminist issues in Pakistan, is Shamsa Jaagir. During her interview with me, Jaagir (personal communication, 9 January 2002) asserted that for the oppressive elements in the society it does not matter how they keep the customs intact. They will do it with whatever means are available: 'Here if it suits them they will use religion for oppression. Otherwise they use social norms. It does not matter what you call it. I mean Islam does not allow honour killing. Now it is social. I mean, even a murder is called something like an honourable thing to do.' (Jaagir, personal communication, 9 January 2002).

In Pakistan honour killing is carried on with what she called 'cultural impunity.' She said that she mentioned the idea of cultural impunity in her report to the United Nations. Honour killing, in her view, is sanctified by law and lack of affirmative action by the governments. 'Adultery?' She asks quizzically and then answers herself, 'You don't get along, you don't get along. I mean, you don't go kill people for that.'

What Jaagir calls 'cultural impunity' is the hegemonic weight of mythic consciousness structures, where tradition is oppressive, and —in this case of honour killing—deadly. The social development of getting divorced, or legal separations between spouses, is a manifestation of the dissociation and atomism that is a concomitant of modernity or rational modes of awareness. The battle lines between the collectivist and the individualist modes of life are clearly drawn.

I asked Jaagir how she views the tension between the rights of the individual and those of the collectivity:

Jaagir: Well, I don't believe anything is for all times. Because some things we did ... people saying we [women] want to rule our lives, we want to have the right to decide our destiny. That is all a part of human rights. As in the South Asian context.

She then mentioned the poetry of Faiz, [16] asking if I had read it.

Jafri: I have been doing it all my life.

Jaagir: So, what is that, what is that? [She gets excited] You read even poetry of people who are activist poets, as I call them, Habib Jalib,[17] 'Aisay dastoor ko subh e baynoor ko mein naheen manta, mein naheen jaanta ('This constitution, this morning of despair, I don't accept, I don't want to have any business with'). What is that? Is it not founded in freedom? And is it not human rights? And there are people, I can count hundreds of people that I know personally in Pakistan who have fought for this struggle without any fear or favour, who have died perhaps not penniless but...and there are people whose thinking, whose vision of what is human rights is far above any of the intellectuals that I have met in the West.[18]

Jafri: Of course. I am not comparing East and West here at all. And I wasn't going ...

Jaagir: And so it is universal.

Jafri: I am elaborating. It is universal ...

Jaagir: Right. Why do I say it is universal? Because when you humiliate a child down the road whether the child is black, red, white whatever, Pakistani, Indian, Jew, Christian, Muslim, you will see the hurt. So it is universal.

Later, talking about the rights of the individual and the collective, Jaagir discusses women as representing individualism and men as the symbol of collectivity, of what she considered oppression.

Jaagir: OK, now when you talk about individual rights against the rights of the community as such. They actually think that the fact that we have not gone forward we are better off than the thirties and forties.

Jafri: Who?

Jaagir: Is because the individual within the community is suppressed and I think it is very important for … to not give those rights to their women. I mean I started all this whole thing in … has to be sacrificed at the altar of collective rights.[19] So, I think there is [a] the role of the state to take individual rights. Secondly, if you look to itself the admiration for somebody who asserted … individual rights are far more. For example, what is this Sassi Panoon, Heer Ranjha? Heer[20] more.

Jafri: 'Heer more…' I could not but agree to such vehemence. But, I agree, she was right.

Jaagir: Heer more! Who is the person, who is the despicable one? It is Kaidoo.[21] And Kaidoo is a despicable man who actually puts societal pressure on her. So, I mean if you look at culture … emotions are always linked to the individual that bucks the collective, in a [situation] where the collective is becoming oppressive. What is that? That is (the) individual that bucks the collective.[22] In a manner, here [meaning in Pakistan] the collective is becoming oppressive. What is that? That is individual rights? What was that, even if you look at the, for example, even our modern leaders. The man who bucked the system or the woman who bucked the system actually held the imagination of the people. So, I am afraid in I understand individual vs. collectivity but when you are in Pakistan women suffer and are not comforted by collectiveness.

Then pointing outside her office where women, mostly poor and not many cheerful, were occupying all the floor space in the waiting room and the spacious corridors, she added: 'Yaqeen karain abhi do bajay (believe me just now by 2 p.m.)' and quickly clarifying in English what she had uttered in Urdu, 'This hall would be full by 2 o'clock. All these women come. Please don't ask how much the families helped them! In trouble, nobody comes to their rescue. The family structures have broken for women. They have broken because there are a lot of narcotics[23] in this country. One out of five men is into narcotics. You see what these women go through!

Once their husbands die, their property is taken away from them. If they are divorced and they go and live in their brother's house, any money they have their brother takes away from them.' And, then, with her hands spread out in a desperate gesture: 'What collective? For the oppressed?'

This echoes Spivak's (1998) warning about the possible repercussions of blunting the efforts of agency by women: 'The possibility of collectivity itself is persistently foreclosed through the manipulation of female agency' (p. 283). The flaunting of collectivity and rhetorical flourishes such as 'one for all and all for one,' in Jaagir's view, are idealized notions that only serve to perpetuate the status quo, which is obviously and brutally loaded in favour of the men. Used as scapegoats for honour and as pawns in the power games that men play among themselves, women are stripped of their resources and are left to fend for themselves.

According to Triandis (1995), Joseph Campbell was initially sympathetic to the collective spirit of the East while he denigrated the individualists of the West, but after his trip to India he changed his mind. The ideal of a collectivist society is a human myth, one of a lost Eden; it is a romantic notion. In Kramer's (personal communication, 2003) view, Campbell suffered from 'orientalism' which is (was) a romantic myth. On his subsequent visits to the East, Campbell discovered—what Jaagri laments in this interview— that often in such societal structures, individuals were ignored, taken advantage of, and expected to serve the group. In requiring conformity to ingroup authorities, collectivism particularly oppressed women.

In Gebser's (1985) view, the ideologies of individualistic and collectivistic societies cannot prevail for too long. In contemporary societies, on the one hand the individual is being driven to increased isolation where the individual him(her)self becomes the clan, while the collective degenerates into mere aggregation. Gebser (1985) asserts that, 'These two conditions, isolation and aggregation, are in fact clear indications that individualism and collectivism have now become deficient' (p. 3).

Dr Tahira Khan, a professor of Women's Studies in Karachi, understands collectivity as represented by the active connivance of cultural, political, and religious forces in the country.

> Whenever women assert their rights to choose, or abused wives attempt to get out of abusive relationships, all the patriarchal coercive forces join hands together to suppress the revolt and to eradicate transgression by using all cultural, religious, and political weapons (Khan, 18 April 1999).

The theme touched on by Jaagri is repeated here: The oppression of the individual woman by the collective culture is represented by 'patriarchal coercive forces.' In Khan's view, when it comes to keeping the woman in her disadvantaged social situation, the men employ every weapon available to them. Pathan (19 August 1991), a political activist, declared at a seminar that, in Pakistan, women have been made into slaves in the name of tradition and will not stand for it any longer. In Pakistan, women's rights activists are articulating a message of defiance of the individual woman in the face of oppressive forces originating in the collectivistic social structure.

THE CONCEPTS OF 'AGENCY' AND 'INTERRUPTION'

Reading the various statements, speeches, articles, and books by prominent feminists in Pakistan and then in my interviews with several women engaged in social struggles in Pakistan, I was repeatedly reminded of the concept of 'agency' and 'interruption' in Western feminist literature. One of my professors[24] was fond of narrating a story about Madeleine Albright, the US Secretary of State during the Clinton administration:

Before she was nominated Secretary of State, Albright was known in more esoteric circles inside the Washington beltway as a respected professor of law and international affairs at Georgetown. In informal settings, she was fond of holding soirees for the exchange of views with the learned and the powerful about issues of the day. Usually not any less accomplished than any of the mandarins in attendance, but often the only woman attendee, Albright noticed herself being regularly ignored, patronized, interrupted, and/or talked over by the men. Being a smart person, she also soon realized that the men who interrupted her to take and relish centre-stage often did not have anything of substance to add to what she had said or had intended to say. She learned that although these were accomplished and smart men, during their acculturation over time in the corridors of power, they had developed bad habits of communication. These men did not care to listen when their women colleagues talked, so they interrupted them.

She developed two concurrent strategies of communication in order to effectively relay her message, *i.e.*, to be heard: First, she started interrupting those men with a loud enough voice and vivid gestures whenever she felt that she had something of substance to contribute; and second, she started to counter-interrupt, *i.e.*, if someone interrupted her while she was in the middle of making a point, she would raise her voice, and respectfully insist that she be allowed to finish first. Soon, the modes of communication in their group changed. Albright managed to disperse power in the room more equitably and for the benefit of all. The result of Albright's strategy was the liberation of both the historically oppressed who had been denied expression, and the oppressor who had historically denied himself the pleasure of listening and possible enrichment. At a micro-level—and instructive in a number of ways—this was a revolution in the way people communicated in those settings. Later on, possibly because of her strategy to be unconventionally assertive and her acquisition of what Reynolds (1998) calls 'agency,' Albright was heard well beyond the group of *rishis* (aficionados of Buddhist texts) in Georgetown.

Reynolds (1998) has explored how 'interruption,' as a feature of conversation, can contribute to the acquisition of "agency." As human beings we learn quickly the lesson of interruption and the way to be heard in the din of the family is to speak louder. In Reynolds' (1998) view, 'Although butting in and yelling louder than anyone else may not be strategies that endure—their effectiveness may be limited to kairotic[25] moments—they can sometimes be satisfactorily interventionalist' (p. 60). The strategy of interruption can be effective only in kairotic moments, *i.e.*, the interrupter must be sensitive to the rhetorical importance of time and place in addition to the juxtaposition of the speaker's and her own power. Even in a modern individualistic society like the United States, most communicative situations—especially domestic ones—do not lend themselves to such interruptions. In collectivistic societies like Pakistan that function in the mythic structures of awareness and where the expectations of roles of conduct for men and women are deeply embedded in the daily cultural life, such strategy will not only be ineffective but can be potentially dangerous for the common woman. However, among the educated and professional women in Pakistan there is a growing awareness of constraints placed on them because of their gender. As demonstrated earlier, a recurrent theme in the representative feminist discourse is that honour killing and other forms of extreme violence are a manifestation of the structurally imposed inequities forced on the women as a gender group. This strand of feminism in Pakistan advocates agency for the women and attempts to interrupt the hegemonic discourses in the country in order to remove the constraints and to facilitate the evolution of new roles for women and new modes of relationships between men and women.

According to Hooks (1989) 'Agents are those who speak as an equal to an authority figure ... daring to disagree' (p. 5). Acquiring agency is a process of developing a capacity to exercise will, to determine the shape of one's own life, and to some extent, play a role in the shaping of one's culture. Interruption is like asserting, one is mindful of one's self-respect and intellectual self-regard. In Reynolds' (1998) view, 'Agency is not simply about finding one's own voice, but also about intervening in discourses of the everyday and cultivating rhetorical tactics that make interruption and resistance an important part of any conversation' (p. 59).

Unlike most of the other people I interviewed, the feminist activists, Jaagir and Khan, casually and as a matter of course, interrupted me whenever they thought it necessary during the interview. For me this communicative style and strategy was a manifestation of their acquired agency, and their understanding of the *kairos* of the moment. This communicative strategy in interpersonal communication is analogous to their activism on the national and even the international stage. This strand of feminism has acquired the education and social savvy to understand the political dynamics of Pakistan and accordingly address it in the streets, the courts of law, seminars, media, and other forums. In a word, they have the intellectual wherewithal to interrupt the national discourse at *kairotic* moments. They have played a large role in bringing the discussion of honour killing to the forefront of the national discussion by effective use of their communication strategies.[26]

A relevant distinction between 'tactics' and 'strategy' is articulated within the Western feminist discourse. In Reynolds' (1998) view:

> Strategies are institutional, operating from a base to calculate or manipulate power relationships, whereas tactics can occur in the absence of a proper locus, in the midst of shifting practices and marginal or multiple sites. Interruption might become part of a tactical rhetoric for marginalized speakers and writers—those who are often interrupted routinely as well as those who do not speak or write form a single location. (p. 59)

Interruption by the disenfranchised can, thus, only be attempted from locales specific to social situations. In de Certeau's (1984) schema, strategy is the calculation of power relationships that becomes possible only when the subject with will and power can be located. In Pakistan's cultural context, only those women who have acquired the ability to distinguish their own place and the place of those women who are brutalized and killed *vis-à-vis* the position of oppressive power can calculate the power relationships in their society. Not every one is equipped to do that. Thus, if the 'educated' and 'sophisticated' feminists have an operation base from which to challenge the status quo, they are strategizing.[27] Women who are totally disenfranchised employ tactics rather than strategy, as de Certeau (1984) says, 'Tactic is an art of the weak' (p. 37).

SUMMARY

This chapter was largely about the schema of individualistic and collectivistic cultures as articulated by communication scholars such as Gebser, Kramer, Triandis, Hofstede, Tonnies, Hui, and Ting-Toomey. In the light of the data, I discussed how the concept of individualistic and collectivistic cultures plays out in Gebser's (1985) scheme of the magic/mythic and mental/rational structures of awareness. For this purpose, I parsed the texts of the statements made by some of the Pakistan senators during the tabling of the motion to condemn honour killing. Additionally, I used my interviews with some feminists, human rights advocates, and public opinion leaders. Finally, I briefly explored the concept of 'agency' and 'interruption' as articulated in Western feminist literature and its possible relevance for the situation of women in Pakistan in general and for honour killing in particular. For this, I demonstrated how only women who have acquired education, skills, and power can grasp the *kairotic* moment and may be in the position to interrupt oppressive conversations or national discourse through the use of what de Certeau (1984) calls 'strategy.' For women with little or no hope of becoming agents, it is not possible to make their presence vivid and can even be dangerous to assert and interrupt.

NOTES

1. Men are sometimes punished but rarely killed for perceived breach of honour by the male members of their clan. This is not to say that they are not sensitive to what is expected of them as social behaviour. The worst stigma that a male member can carry in Pakistan society is that of passivity in a homosexual relationship and cowardice. Often and interestingly, as in certain idioms, the two are synonymous. In certain tribal clans, breach of a taboo such as audibly farting can doom a man. A close friend of mine who was an officer in the Pakistan Army astonished and amused me once by telling me how his paternal grandfather had imbibed in him the importance of the control of rectal muscles—the ultimate defence line, so to say—in a man. The patriarch would narrate (interestingly, only to young boys) how once at a dinner spread as a family elder was about to bring a

morsel to his mouth he could not hold or muffle what turned out to be a resounding fart. All men at the dinner heard it but such was the resonance of shame at the moment that not a head lifted, no eye contacts were made. The obviously dishonoured elder deliberately brought the morsel back to the plate instead of taking it to his mouth where it was headed, got up from the floor, and quietly left the all-male dining ritual. He was never heard of again. Ever. Having atoned for the 'weak' and thus dishonourable moment by a lifetime of self-imposed banishment from the clan, he was now mentioned as a hero in the clan's mythologizing about sacrifices that a man has to offer for the sake of honour.

2. According to Gebser (1985), 'archaic is derived from the Greek *arche* which means inception, origin' (p. 43).

3. It may be pertinent to point out that my last (family) name denotes my lineage from Mohammad Jaffer bin Mohammad Baqir. Indiscretions notwithstanding, *Jafris* (Arabic for 'Jaferites') claim to be the direct descendents of Jaffer who was a grandson of a grandson of the Prophet Muhammad. According to http://members.fortunecity.com/masoom110/TRUEISLAM/id25.html, apart from being the sixth imam of Islam, he was the major scholar, chemist, theologian, hermeneutist of his time. Among his students was the eminent chemist Jabir bin Hayyan who invented Aqua Regia, Sulfuric Acid, and Nitric Acid. As an example of the functioning of collective societies, I want to add that in my family there is never a day when the names and deeds of several ancestors are not mentioned. A child's education begins with mentioning, committing to memory, and writing down with a sense of religious gravity the names and deeds of, yes, male ancestors.

4. Faisalabadi meaning 'of Faisalabad.' It would be considered absurd if not outright hilarious, for example, if Jerry Falwell, in an individualistic and highly mobile culture like the U.S., were to be known as Jerry Falwell Charlotsvillian.

5. Borrowed from Maslow's hierarchy of needs.

6. Embedded in the pithy linguistic construct is the understanding that the three—*zan, zar, aur zameen*—are equal commodities for the man.

7. Sharif and Bhutto each served two terms as prime minister of Pakistan. Leghari was the president of Pakistan during part of the 1990s.

8. Rhetorically, *haj* is a revered God term in any Islamic country since performing *haj* is one of the five fundamental duties of a Muslim along with reciting the *kalma*, prayers, fasting and alms. If someone, for example, dies or is killed in an accident or a plane crash on the way to *haj*, (s)he is said to be fortunate to have taken the short-cut to God's promised heavens.

9. Lahore has a fascinating hold on the Pakistani psyche. On the one hand, the city is centre of culture and education etc., while on the other, it is considered the epitome of freedom and the risky and group-defying

behaviour that freedom can trigger. In folk stories and songs, Lahore is often mentioned as a place where the degenerate go for a 'good time.' (As in the present-day New York and New Orleans—and several other 'happening' places—Lahore is also where *fitna* resides.)

10. Among other meanings Feroze (2001) translates *sharafat* as 'nobility,' 'gentlemanliness,' etc. The root word for *sharafat* is *sharaf* on the meaning of which is 'honour.' Lang (2000), for example, doing research on honour killing in the Middle East, titles her dissertation: 'Sharaf Politics: Constructing male prestige in Israeli-Palestinian society.'

11. *Bachi* means 'a little girl.' Feminists have argued that the use of such terms for grown up women (a mother of two in this case) is infantilizing and condescending and thus, rhetorically, a means of oppression by men. By branding Samia—a mother of two—as 'little girl,' the senator here implies that the woman was mentally incapable of knowing right from wrong or of making decisions for herself.

12. This is the exact way in which it appeared in the newspaper. He means that the society stands on the strong edifice of archaic (here meaning 'seasoned,' 'tried,' and 'dependable') morality supported by religion, etc.

13. The use of distancing rhetoric is glaring by the use of 'their' for national and international institutions such as the Human Rights Organization of Pakistan and Non Governmental Organizations. Yousufzai, clearly a Pakistani, does not want to have any truck with 'them' pollutants.

14. He was talking about the United Nations Convention on the Elimination of all forms of Discrimination Against Women (UN CEDAW), ratified by Pakistan in 1996. Under CEDAW, the Pakistani government is responsible for changing attitudes and practices contributing to violations of women's rights.

15. As a manifestation of what Kramer (2000) calls cultural fusion. Kentucky Fried Chicken's best selling item in its two outlets in Karachi, Pakistan, is not anything on its conventional menu found in the West, but a chicken sandwich (called 'the Zinger') that has peppers and spices added in order to cater to the local palate. On the other hand, some Pakistanis who usually had more conventional and elaborate lunches are finding sandwiches to be a more elegant, less messy, lunch. With this process of cultural fusion, then, new foods, languages, modes of communication, and attitudes evolve. Apart from Maasoom, I talked about this with the manager of the KFC at Zaib-un-Nissa Street, Karachi.

16. A companion of Neruda, Hikmat, and other communist poets who gained eminence in the cold war era, Faiz is regarded as the foremost poet of the Urdu language of the latter half of 20th century. A recipient of the Lenin Peace Prize, Faiz championed the downtrodden all over the globe in his writings.

17. Often imprisoned for his defiance, Jalib (1928–92) was a revolutionary poet in Pakistan who, in the face of brutal odds, fought for the rights of the disenfranchised and the poor.

18. In the heat of her polemic, Jaagir's focus is a little blurred here but she wants to clarify that the idea of human rights is not one that is or needs to be borrowed from the West. Indeed, in her view, our own home-grown poets and activists have articulated it eloquently.

19. Animated as she is, Jaagir is speaking rapidly and both her speech and ideas are getting jumbled. She means that she had started the movement for women's rights in Pakistan and to take away some power from men. In this, she wants the state to play an activist role.

20. Jaagir is evoking the two well-known folklores of Punjabi/Sindhi culture in which the protagonists were women. For their love, *Heer* and *Sassi* defied the collective, the oppressive structures of society, and paid with their lives. Considered the apotheosis of the heroic, they are much eulogized in epic poetry in regional languages. When Jaagir says '*Heer*' more' assertively, she seeks my agreement about *Heer* being the 'hero' of the epic rather than the man, *Ranjha*, that she loved.

21. *Kaidoo* is the lame villain of the tale. As a representative of the status quo, *Kaidoo* sabotages the love affair with his unctuous guiles and hypocrisy.

22. Though a modernist, Jaagir summons national mythology to her defence. In folk tales, it is the individual who fights against entrenched oppression who is usually seen as the hero, not the defender of the status quo. In the West, the Lone Ranger and the cowboy are good examples of such mythologizing.

23. Elsewhere, she pointed out (and there is plenty of research and empirical evidence) that the overwhelming single reason for the permeation of society with narcotics was the Afghan war of the 80s in which Pakistan, with the active support of the CIA, played a key role. Most of the heroin smuggled to the world from Afghanistan passed through Pakistan. People in Pakistan, where liquor had been banned a little earlier (1977), took to heroin with uncommon ardour.

24. Kathleen Welch, with whom I studied rhetoric during the course of my graduate work at the University of Oklahoma, 2002.

25. According to Helsley (1996), *kairos* means 'right timing and proper measure—directly related to the rhetorical importance of time, place, speaker, and audience, the proper and knowledgeable analysis of these factors, and the faculty of using the proper means in a particular context to arrive at a belief. For the Pythagoreans, *kairos* is one of the laws of the universe referring to the balance between the thesis and antithesis' (p. 371). Kinneavy (1980) argues to include *kairos* in literary and philosophical hermeneutics. Among other disciplines like tagmemics and poststructuralist literary criticism, *kairos* is implicitly evidenced in speech communication and in the work of Freud, Burke, and Hirsch (Kinneavy, 1980, p. 104).

26. The way we communicate may be seen as a series of habits we acquire in our lives and attitudes that have been culturally embedded in us over the course of time. After listening to the interview recordings several times, I realized that instead of putting a question and waiting for the response, I would often try to make the question-asking an occasion to obliquely express the importance of my work and my familiarity with the literature. Sometimes, instead of trying to listen to what they were saying, I started lecturing. These were intelligent, serious, and accomplished women who were engaged and committed to a number of causes. Naturally, they would have no patience with my forays into solipsism and would do to me what Albright did to similar men—afflicted with a sense of self-importance—in Georgetown. They expressed their impatience with gestures that were sometimes not too subtle—like thumping the table and shaking their heads in disagreement—and often with the Albright-manoeuvre: simply raising their voice and without being obnoxious talking over my ramble if I continued unnecessarily. In retrospect, I see this interruption during interpersonal discourse analogous to their interruption of the national discourse, emblematic of their heroic struggle against tremendous odds and unprecedented cultural pressures. As representatives of a historically oppressed group, they are compelled to raise their voice to come out of the submersion and to be heard amidst the number of smug and oppressive hegemonic discourses.

27. Interestingly derived from the Greek *strategos* meaning 'military general.'

6

Legal and Feminist Discourse

In order to understand the range between outrage and condemnation on one hand and acquiescence and advocacy of honour killing on the other, it is important to parse the various discourses in Pakistan that deal with the phenomenon. The legal, political, religious, philosophic—in short ideological—forms of discourses that people utilize and the foundational texts through which they seek justification for honour killing are all sources of understanding the act. In this chapter, I shall look at some of the representative texts of the various discursive communities in Pakistan in order to locate power and how it influences and prescribes modes of conduct in society. I shall also demonstrate the inherent difficulties of viewing women, religious orthodoxy, or sometimes even members of the same political party, as a monolithic discourse community mutually exclusive from others.

Discourse communities are organic units, with constituent elements that often find sympathy for other such organic units; conversely, these discourses also attract elements from other discourse communities. Under the larger cultural setting, then, the defining aspects of these discursive formations are forever shifting. Still, it is important to study these discourses because, according to Foucault (1980), it is in discourse that power and knowledge come together to potentially spur action. Honour killing is clearly an act where one group exercises brute power over another. For this, inspiration is garnered and power derived from specific discourses. It follows that those who interpret these discourses wield power and play a role in the shifting 'conscious system of ideas and beliefs' (Williams, 1990, p. 109). As these ideas and beliefs jostle with each other and diffuse in the society, the various discursive formations gain and lose—to borrow from Gramsci—'hegemonic power.'

THE STATE AND THE JUDICIARY

In Pakistani society, the judiciary plays a pivotal role in articulating and enforcing rules of conduct for its citizens. The judiciary derives its legitimacy and power from the constitution. The Constitution of Pakistan guarantees gender equality in several articles. For example, Article 25 states: 'All citizens are equal before law and are entitled to equal protection of law.' Article 27 is unequivocal about the rights of citizens: 'There shall be no discrimination on the basis of sex alone.' Apart from the constitution, Pakistan is also obligated to defend international rights, those of the UN for example, of all individuals. Of the international human rights treaties relevant to the issue of honour killing, Pakistan has ratified the UN Convention on the Elimination of all forms of Discrimination Against Women (CEDAW), as discussed earlier.

In this section, using judgments in certain cases of honour killing, I shall demonstrate how, in spite of these codifications, the traditional and the structurally inbuilt iniquities toward women persist. The various judgments in cases of honour killing are messages that are sent to the community about how the state views their conduct. The state, rather obviously, affects the conduct of its citizens. However, the perspectival legal documents are not the only discourse that define the status of women in Pakistan. To varying degrees, the elements of the deficient mythic awareness also contribute to it. Thus certain tribal codes, interpretation of religious injunctions, Indo–Pakistan judicial traditions, customary traditions, etc., all interplay to create the existing conditions. Any advantage or opportunity offered by some legislation is often cancelled, overlooked, or finessed by some traditional imperative in the courts of law. Judges, after all, are part of the society in which they live and reflect many of its cultural values, moral norms, and prejudices.

At this point, it is important to make note of the law of *Qisas* [1]and *Diyat* [2] recommended by the Council of Islamic Ideology over and above the constitution of Pakistan. These laws cover offences relating to physical injury, manslaughter, and murder and, according to these, the offense is not considered as directed against the legal order of the state but against the person of the victim (Sheikh, personal communication, 31 December 2000). Clearly, this approach to criminal offences reinforces assumptions regarding the private nature of murder within the family. Thus a clear message is sent to the community that killing of a family member is a private affair and has to be taken care of domestically. The message also implies that prosecution and legal redress are not inevitable but negotiable. According to Supreme Court lawyer Jilani (personal communication, 15 April 2003):

> The law really facilitates such killings. Killings are private offences, against the individual, not the state, so who will bring and pursue the charges of murder? If the father or brother kills a woman, the family of the girl will not pursue the case, as in their eyes no wrong has been done …There is no chance of bringing the killer to book …The prosecution case collapses on almost all the scenarios of an honour killing: In such cases there is no aggrieved party to pursue the case, society as a whole approves of the killing and usually there are no prosecution witnesses as nobody testifies against a family member. Since the killing takes place in a family context, forgiveness, voluntary or otherwise, is almost inevitable. If a brother kills a sister on grounds of honour, her guardian, her father can forgive his son.

The state, thus, in its judicial discourse presents obstacles to full redress of honour killing in Pakistan. The promulgation of the ordinance of *qisas* and *diyat* was a message articulated by the State that was apparently not lost on the male members of the community. Indeed, according to Jahan (January 1999), 'After the ordinance, the number of family members accused of killing women registered a phenomenal rise. Perhaps the possibility to circumvent the defective law accounts for this change in the pattern of maintaining family honour'. (p. 14)

The interface of the mythical and the mental modes of consciousness was evidenced when Justice Sabihuddin Ahmed, Justice of the Sindh High Court, told Amnesty International

(1999) that in reflecting and upholding traditional concepts of rights, the judiciary in Pakistan was forsaking an important role—that of reform and progress in the area of personal liberty. In his view, courts can either choose to reflect existing and broadly accepted norms of society or they can use the law as an instrument of change.

Following are some judgments from courts of law in Pakistan that exemplify the messages that the judiciary is sending to the community. The struggle for ascendancy between the deficient but still powerful mythical strain and the Western perspectival is ever present. By viewing these judgments one also understands how violence is sometimes woven and normalized in cultures. As Galtung (1990) puts it 'Cultural violence makes direct and structural violence look, even feel, right—or at least not wrong'. (p. 291). A scan of these cases, cited in an Amnesty International Report (1999), provides an idea of how the acts of direct violence as they are absorbed and legitimized and thus gradually rendered acceptable in society.

In 1983, a man, Moula Bux, killed his fiancée and her family because they had refused his demand for an early marriage. His death sentence was commuted to life imprisonment by the court on grounds that there were mitigating circumstances and that the crime was committed due to a family dispute; the appellant felt his honour was injured and this provoked him to resort to violence. The court explicitly took into account the fact that the appellant belonged to the Brohi tribe and was vulnerable to impulses that tend to injure their peculiar ideas of respect and honour.[3]

In 1992, a high court argued that the 'impact of provocation on human frailty is to be judged in the context of social position and environment of the person concerned. The restraint which is generally shown by sophisticated persons used to modern living is hardly to be expected in the case of a villager who still regards his wife as his personal property and chattel.'[4]

While hearing the bail application of Liaqat Ali who had gravely injured his sister and stabbed to death the man he found with her, the Lahore High Court in 1994 was told by the petitioner's counsel that, 'in an Islamic society a person found to indulge in adultery

served to be finished there and then. Indeed such
more of a religious duty that an offence.' According to
nternational (1999), 'The judge reportedly responded:
cie, I am inclined to agree with the counsel".' (Amnesty
International, 1999, p. 56)

In another case, the Lahore High Court commuted three death
sentences to life imprisonment on grounds of damage to a man's
honour. With the help of two male relatives, Mohammad Sharif
had killed his wife, the man she had gone to live with, and that
man's father. The court concluded that this case did not involve
sudden and severe provocation but nevertheless had mitigating
circumstances. The judge ruled that, 'As such, their family honour
has been attacked and injured to an alarming extent and this
brought shame to them which continuously egged them on to
avenge their grievance and to restore … their family honour …
certainly provided a mitigating circumstance.'[5]

These examples show how deeply entrenched the mythic
structures of consciousness are in Pakistani society. They also
demonstrate what Foucault (1995) calls 'the gap between the laws
and the real practice of the courts' (p. 15). Even lawyers and judges,
professionals trained in the modern legal ways, found it impossible
to resist the pull of their traditions and culture. Women are
structurally pinned in subordinate positions by custom, tradition,
and law, where much of the endemic violence, even killing, is often
considered normal behaviour. With the implementation of
retroactive laws, the notion of defilement of male honour seems to
have extended beyond perceived sexual misconduct into perceived
defiance of male control. The judiciary, through its judgments in
honour killing cases, has sent messages to the community that have
not discouraged the future perpetrators of such crimes. According
to Amnesty International Report (1999),

> While the media coverage of honour killings has no doubt increased,
> leading to more such cases being reported, the real incidence,
> particularly of economically motivated killings of women concealed as
> honour killings, appears to have gone up as well. The sense of
> righteousness manifest in the way killings are carried out in broad

daylight, sometimes in public places in front of witnesses, appears to have grown, too. (p. 32)

It is clear that in spite of the laws of the land prescribed by the rational modes of awareness, the mythic holds sway. Sometimes under pressure from the traditionalists and occasionally unable to rise above their own prejudices, the judges often tend to send messages to the community that reinforce discriminatory norms against women. In Shaheed's (1998) view:

> Since the interpretation of law cannot be detached from the specific cultural context in which it is located, norms and accepted practices profoundly affect the application and interpretation of law ... In societies in which the concept of honour killings is socially validated, the formal legal system will reflect this validation ... in spite of the textual provisions of the law. (p. 65)

THE 'TACTICAL' STRAND OF FEMINIST DISCOURSE

There are some strong emerging feminist voices in Pakistan that contribute to the national discourse. In the course of this document I have made use of my interviews with some of these women along with essays and articles by women who are professors, writers, lawyers, and activists. As subalterns,[6] these women have trained themselves to be versed in the language of the oppressor; they have acquired agency and are retaliating by public demonstrations, voicing their views on the national media, and taking up cudgels in law courts.

As a Pakistani who understands the local cultures to some extent, I found the voice of a 14-year-old Sindhi girl to represent the essential cultural situation of her kind. Her poem in which she expresses her fear of being potentially declared a *kari* is also an interruption in the hegemonic discourse in the confines of the community in which she lives. It may be a weak interruption in the face of structurally embedded oppression, but it is an eloquent one; and although we only have access to its English version recorded by Attiya Dawood (1999) the words deserve our attention if for no other reason than Brodsky's (1986) comment about the power of the poem in the specific context of this study: 'A poem is not a news report, and often a poem's tragic music alone informs us of what is happening more precisely than a detailed description can' (p. 196). I am fully aware of the limitations of all translations. Benjamin's (1968) position that 'Fidelity in the translation of individual words can almost never fully reproduce the meaning they have in the original' (p. 78) and the comment attributed to Ezra Pound that in translating poetry the only thing that is left behind is poetry, fully resonates with me. In our circumstance, however, the translation—by nature ideational—will have to do because we are concerned with the idea and not aesthetics of expression here. This poem carries a deeper resonance, a more pointed immediacy, than the opinions and theorizings of intellectuals, journalists, jurists, politicians, and activists. I reproduce Attiya Dawood's (1999) translation into English of the coarse Sindhi dialect of an 'illiterate' girl:

> What is there to my body?
> Is it studded with diamonds or pearls?
> My brother's eyes forever follow me.
> My father's gaze guards me all the time,
> Stern, angry.
> Then why do they make me labour in the fields?
> All day long, bear the heat and the sun,
> Sweat and toil and we tremble all day long,
> Not knowing who may cast a look upon us.
> We stand accused, and condemned to be declared *kari*
> And murdered (Dawood, 1999, p. 3).

This example of the tactical (de Certeau, 1984) strain of Pakistani feminism was written by this Sindhi girl[7] who epitomizes the marginalized and the brutalized. More importantly, this poem expresses the indomitable nature of the human spirit. In contrast to her fellow feminists (and natural allies), she is innocent of rhetorical skills and legal expertise—the ways of the world. In all likelihood, she is unaware of their efforts to thwart oppression, or even whether such efforts are possible. She is a representative of an oral culture, without access to the written word. On the other hand, in her lack of urban sophistication, she is embodied emotion and is all feeling; as in all art, the semantic distance between what she felt and suffered and what she expressed is reduced. It is only through the chance discoveries by journalists like Dawood that she can unwittingly contribute to the national discourse about honour killing. Indeed, in the process, she becomes identified with the phenomenon. It will be hard to speculate what effect her expression may have within her community where this girl is so acutely aware of the savageries, including brutal death, that lie in wait for her.

For me the voice of the anonymous girl represents a discursive community. A relatively unheralded, mute, and brutally oppressed strand among the various feminisms[8] in Pakistan, but one that needs to be brought to light. In his interview with Brochier, Foucault (1980), too, emphasizes the importance of methodically studying what he calls the usually 'unseen':

> But to make visible the unseen can also mean a change of level, addressing oneself to a layer of material which hitherto had no pertinence for history and which had not been recognized as having any moral, aesthetic, political or historical value. (pp. 50–51)

If the voice of the educated and conscientious women in Pakistan articulates and theorizes the plight of the brutalized women on national and international forums, the voice of this anonymous poet is the sigh from what Spivak (1998) has called the 'silenced centre of the circuit marked out by this epistemic violence, men and women among the illiterate peasantry, the tribals, the lowest strata' (p. 283). Because the purpose of this work is to develop an understanding of the phenomenon of honour killing in Pakistan, this sigh contributes to our task of 'measuring silences'[9] (Mechery, 1978, p. 87) by making us feel the resonance of the silence around the threat of being declared *kari* under which a 14-year-old girl lives.

Of note in Spivak's (1998) articulation is the essential and inescapable heterogeneity in the composition of this strand of the subaltern. In Pakistan's national context, like the poor girl, her brothers and father are also the perennially marginalized of the society. Existing at the farthest removes from any amenities of modern life, as a community these people are the true subalterns: voiceless, resourceless, powerless, without any education, and with little hope, they are often invisible. And as a cruel irony, the men so ruthlessly oppressed as a subaltern class with their women, also happen to be the brutal oppressors of their women-kin as articulated in the girl's poem. In theorizing their social situation and ascertaining their discursive formation, such irresolvable conflicts and inbuilt ambiguities can prove intractable, because in spite of their ingroup feuds and blood spilling, they all constitute the same subaltern class. What Spivak (1998) considers the task of deconstruction—to provide an account of this shifting relationship— can also be considered, in this case, the task of hermeneutics. In the context of colonial/imperial[10] discourse, Spivak (1998) memorably calls the female subaltern 'doubly effaced' (p. 287). This poet, then, is 'doubly effaced' because, already existing at the fringe of human resources, she is being further brutalized by her kinsmen, by those who should be her natural allies in the struggle of life. Spivak (1998) points out that:

> It is, rather, that, both as object of colonialist historiography[11] and as subject of insurgency, the ideological construction of gender keeps the male dominant. If, in the context of colonial production, the subaltern has no history and cannot speak, the subaltern as female is even more deeply in the shadow. (p. 287)

In order to understand the voice of this and other discourse communities in Pakistan that affect rules of conduct linked with honour killing, Gramsci's concept of 'hegemony,' his work on subaltern classes (1998), used in conjunction with Foucault's notion of 'discourse' can provide a useful theoretical framework. To reiterate, Foucault (1990) takes discourse to be a series of discontinuous segments with unstable and varied tactical function. He warns: 'We must not imagine a world of discourse divided between accepted discourse and excluded discourse, or between the dominant discourse and the dominated one; but as a multiplicity of discursive elements that can come into play in various strategies' (p. 100).

Because Gramsci (1998) created a most astonishing opus of political theory without any referential material and on improvised stationary during imprisonment under the Italian Fascist regime, it was left to later scholars to compile and edit his work. Thus the title 'Selections from prison notebooks.' A recurrent term in his writing is 'hegemony' which he uses to elucidate the constant struggle for domination by the various groups in a society. For Gramsci (1998), power is expressed through the direct control (*dirigere*: direct, lead, rule) but also through something less formal but more total (*egomania*: hegemony).[12] The concept of 'hegemony' refers to the cultural dynamic by which a group claims and sustains a leading position in social life. Williams (1990) interprets 'rule' as something expressed in direct political forms which in times of crisis have the potential to take the form of 'effective coercion' (p. 108). Hegemony, on the other hand, consists of interlocking active social and cultural forces. Williams (1990) explains:

> Hegemony is ... a lived system of meanings and values—constitutive and constituting—which, as they are experienced as practices appear as reciprocally confirming. It thus constitutes a sense of reality for most people in the society...beyond which it is very difficult for most members of the society to move ... It is ... in the strongest sense a 'culture' but a culture which has also to be seen as the lived dominance and domination of particular classes. (p. 110)

Although a Marxist, Gramsci (1998) used 'classes' in a broader sense than had been used in the narrower economic-based Marxist literature. For him, the concept of hegemony had to be looked at as a process; it included and went beyond both 'culture' and 'ideology.' As Spivak (1998) explains, 'Gramsci's work on the "subaltern classes" extends the class-position/class-consciousness argument ... he is concerned with the intellectual's role in the subaltern's cultural and political movement into the hegemony' (p. 283). In Pakistan, for example, with a population of about 130 million and a literacy rate of approximately 39 per cent, people who read the English newspaper constitute a specific 'class' in the Gramscian sense. This will not preclude the membership of those individuals in other classes or discursive formations but, being exposed to certain kinds of information not available to a vast majority, they will belong to a certain discourse community— probably with a vigorous ongoing internal debate. Thus exposed to specific modes of articulation as a discursive community, they will be likely to view gender inequities or honour killing in different ways than those without access to that media.

Similarly, urban Pakistani women educated in the Western ways and curricula represent a different set of interests—apart from the obvious overlap about legal rights and such—from the impoverished rural women represented by the above mentioned 14-year-old poet. Additionally, there is an ongoing, well articulated, and serious debate about the role and position of women in the light of the Quran and other classic Islamic texts among the women in the forefront of the feminist movement in Pakistan.

Sometimes in spite of a vast commonality of interests it is still not possible to pin individuals down in a certain discourse formation or Gramscian class. The multi-dimensionality of individuals and the complex and often conflicting nature of their various interests impedes such attempts. What Tinh says about categories is true about Gramscian classes: '...despite our desperate, eternal, attempts to separate, contain, and mend, categories always leak' (as quoted in Ede, et al., 1995, p. 438). This is not different from other movements across the globe. This has led Warhol and Herndl (1996) to argue the use of *Feminisms* instead of 'Feminism' as an acknowledgement of the diversity of opinion and motivation within the movement:

> From the outside, feminism may appear monolithic, unified, or singularly definable ... But, actually, there is a multiplicity of approaches and assumptions inside the movement. While this variety can lead to conflict and competition, it can also be the source of movement, vitality, and genuine learning. Such diversity—if fostered, as it has been in some feminist thought—can be a model for cultural heterogeneity. (p. x)

RELIGIONISTS/TRADITIONALISTS AS A DISCURSIVE COMMUNITY

Similarly, we may be tempted to paint with the same broad brush 'fundamentalists,' 'traditionalists,' or 'religionists' if we are not alert to the ideological clefts within. The various religious orators and mullahs whom I interviewed belong to one or the other ideologically nuanced religious faction. On Pakistan's political landscape, the recently triumphant MMA (*Muttahida Majlis-e-Amal*, United Congress for Action), for example, is a coalition of six different religious parties— that in the past have often been daggers-drawn at each other[13]—in Pakistan, united for the purposes of elections. MMA's interpretations of the sacred texts will determine the laws governing the conduct and position of women in society. Again, while the stipulation of such classes has some validity for analytical purposes, one must always keep in perspective the internal differences and inconsistencies of vision within those discursive formations (Foucault, 1980) or classes. These differences and inconsistencies, as components of concepts, possibly find sympathy and thus alliances, elsewhere, forever forming new Foucauldian discursive formations—all struggling for hegemony in a Gramscian conceptualizing of the social universe.

On the question of honour killing, I could not find a single statement of any Islamic scholar of any sect that overtly condoned the act. There were expressions of sympathy for tradition and culture in some interviews, speeches, editorials, and transcripts of seminars but there were no endorsements for the act. The one exception was the *mullah* at the Islamabad mosque[14] who seemed to have been carried away in the presence of his protégés. But he, too, publicly agreed that the killing of women was against the teachings of Islam. At a seminar arranged by a religious magazine *Ausaf* (Hameed, 20 August 1999) various religious leaders addressed questions about honour killing. None provided evidence of religious tolerance for honour killing. Yousuf declared that, 'Honour killing has nothing to do with Islam. Whenever Muslims want to hide their ignorance, they bring up Islam to give it a bad name. Islam is a religion of total peace and love' (as quoted in

Hameed, p. 8). According to Rehman, 'All said, murder is murder. In Islam, no human being has a right to kill another even in retaliation. All crimes should be dealt with under the law of the land. As a Muslim, nobody has a right to kill another' (as quoted by Hameed, p. 9). Thus the custodians of traditions such as honour killing feel compelled to draw on Islam to justify their crimes. Discussing the social injustices meted out to the women in Pakistan, Kamal and Khan (1997) explain:

> In Pakistan, many of the inequities that the women are subjected to are laid at the door of 'Islam.' Much of the debate on women in Pakistan is being waged by male religious leaders on the one hand and Pakistani feminists (mostly women) on the other. This debate, is therefore, focused on 'Women and Islam,' rather than on women within specific...Pakistani contexts...The often stronger role of traditional and customary laws in shaping the lives of women is only recently beginning to be recognized. (p. 2)

SHIFTING ALLIANCES IN THE PAKISTAN SENATE

During the rowdy senate session (the 96th session, as discussed earlier) which surprisingly failed to pass a resolution condemning Samia's killing, the shifting alliances in the Pakistan senate were also manifested. The resolution was tabled by an opposition senator Iqbal Haider of PPP (Pakistan People's Party). PPP is considered to be a liberal party with a relatively egalitarian agenda. Especially with Benazir Bhutto (a woman—presently in exile) as the leader, the party is ostensibly sympathetic to women's causes. Initially, twenty-four senators from both sides of the aisle had agreed to support the motion, but eventually only four voted for it. Apart from the PPP, the ANP (Awami National Party) has historically been a secular party. Senator Bilour of ANP, whose performance in the senate about honour killing has been already mentioned in this document at length, proudly presented his party's secular credentials while pleading the case for the perpetrators of the killing.

What really surprised the senators (immediately) and the intelligentsia (later) was the attitude and rhetoric of senior senator

Ajmal Khattak of ANP. Having cultivated and secured a reputation as the apotheosis of the progressive and secular poet/ intellectual/ statesman—someone who had, among other Cold War battles, fought alongside Castro and Che Guevara in Bolivia and had been a frequent guest in Moscow—Khattak was expected to strongly condemn honour killing. Instead, he chose to lecture the senators on the concept of honour in the *traditions* of (his) Pakhtun society. Additionally, he sought to derive legitimacy by evoking vocabulary from the sacred Islamic texts. Khattak's friend, the leading progressive Urdu poet Ahmed Nadim Qasimi, (13 September 1999) expressed dismay at Khattak's shift in alliance: 'When I heard that Ajmal Khattak has joined the ranks of those who consider honour killing of women as valid, I felt that a piece of the sky has shattered with a scream.' Haider (10 September 1999) pointed out that Khattak had aligned himself with the feudal and tribal forces of his province, forces that he had considered his antithesis throughout his life. He was also accused of seeking support from the so-called fundamentalists by evoking sanctified terms.[15] The supreme irony of the incident is that Asfandyar Wali Khan, the leader of ANP, a Khattak protégé, addressed a human rights rally and strongly condemned the practice. The surprising fissures and the unlikely alliances in the Pakistan senate demonstrated that no discursive formation is forever complete. Nor is it cast in stone.

What many members of the intelligentsia (such as Haider, Qasmi, and the feminists) did not fully grasp in Ajmal Khattak's valorising of honour was the latent power of tradition. Tradition, as a dormant mythic power, especially in collectivist societies (magic and mythic worlds), provides the defining contours of the individual's personality and is capable of pre-empting rationalizing. Feeling at one with their tradition, individuals in such worlds can reflexively leap to its defence and continuity. So strong is their sense of identification and unity with tradition that the conduct of their life is inseparable from their tradition. Ahmed (7 September 1999) expresses this sentiment when he declares that 'betraying the tradition [of honour killing] is like declaring war on one's own family, society, and tribe.' Yousufzai (6 May 1999) also echoes similar sentiment when he declares, 'True-blooded *Pakhtuns* would

not allow some bodies to dismantle the most revered assets of
Pakhtu and *Pakhtunwali* in the garb of feminism and human
rights.' In different words, Jan (24 August 1999) is expressing the
same emotion when he says that, 'Due to the imported ideologies,
we are fast losing our normative ideologies.' Traditions are the
fountainhead of what Jan calls 'normative consciousness.' Williams
(1990) points out the error of viewing tradition as an inert and
historicized segment of a social structure. On the contrary, Williams
(1990) asserts:

> Tradition is in practice the most evident expression of the dominant
> and hegemonic pressures and limits ... indeed it is the most powerful
> practical means of incorporation. What we have to see is not just 'a
> tradition' but a *selective tradition*: an intentionally selective version of
> a shaping past and a pre-shaped present, which is then powerfully
> operative in the process of social and cultural definition and
> identification. (p. 114)

It is important to note here that even though Williams (1990)
underscores the role of tradition in the social and cultural
churnings, his remains a perspectival version of tradition. Lived-
tradition, which is what motivates and triggers the social actions of
the vast majority of illiterates and those who tacitly or otherwise
support honour killing, is not selected by some meta-criteria; it is
the self and the extended self as collective identity. A Pushtun does
as a Pushtun is.

The idea of honour is embedded in the past and tradition; thus
it is mythic and defies reason. Aristotle (1954), the epitome of the
emerging perspectival awareness of his time, demonstrates the yet
vital mythic dimension in his thought when, discussing honour and
nobility, he says that 'Things that deserve to be remembered are
noble ... so are the things that continue even after death those
which are always attended by honour ... all actions are noble ... if
they are worthy of his ancestors' (p. 60).

As can be seen, such shifts in alliances and power are an organic
feature of societies. Said's (1998) reading of Gramsci points toward
the distinction between civil and political society and how power
and domination is realized through them. While civil society

consists of voluntary cultural affiliations such as schools, clubs, sports activities, families, and fraternities, etc., political society consists of the more coercive and formal aspects of the structures of society such as the army, the police, institutions such as Homeland Security and other bureaucracies. The role of such elements that make up the political is direct domination. Said (1998) explains:

> Culture, of course, is to be found operating within civil society, where the influence of ideas, of institutions, and of other persons works not through domination but by what Gramsci calls consent. In any society not totalitarian, then, certain cultural forms predominate over others, just as certain ideas are more influential than others; the form of this cultural leadership is what Gramsci has identified as *hegemony*, an indispensable concept for any understanding of cultural life. (p. 1280)

The deriving of rhetorical strength by Ajmal Khattak from the use of a culturally sanctified term or the summoning of traditional 'values' by other representatives of the various discursive communities points toward what is hegemonic in Pakistan. In the Islamic Republic of Pakistan, where more than 97 percent of the people are Muslims even the ostensibly secular have to keep the badge of religion flashing. Senator Iqbal Haider, for example, repeatedly asserted during the senate proceedings that the reason he was tabling the motion to condemn honour killing was that the practice was against the principles of Islam. There is a constant and palpable effort by the representatives of all discursive communities to align the Islamic teachings with the deeper traditions even when they are clearly at loggerheads. As demonstrated earlier, for the defence of honour killing, the rhetoric of the sacred texts is mythologized and summoned at the service of supporting the pre-Islamic structures of the culture. The Quran and other religious texts, thus become contested spaces between the mythic and the mental modes of awareness. Honour killing, which demonstrably predates Islam, belongs to the lower dimensions of consciousness where things and people are more identical and less fragmented. The blind influence of beliefs in behaviour such as honour killing is strong in the magic and the mythic realm. Faced with the more perspectival (rationally structured) legal veneer of Islam, people of the mythic awareness reflexively want to co-opt the Islamic texts to fit with their deeper consciousness structures of awareness. Faced with the dilemma, instead of foreswearing their centuries-old traditions and behaviour and conforming to the Quran, people expect the Quran to conform to their ancient norms. They are helpless under the overwhelming force of tradition. Honour killing is a way of life for them, the only way they know of to address a particular cathartic situation. In communication terms, it is a form of messaging. The various defences of honour killing are meta-messages that emerge in reaction to the dialectic of foreign critique. This struggle has occurred with other religions and traditions also. In such situations people feel compelled to make the two match, and even become co-supportive and implicated.

WOMEN AND ISLAMIC TEXTS

As briefly mentioned earlier, the Quran is a series of revelations that were divulged to Prophet Muhammad. These revelations, often experienced as a response to a specific social conundrum, are called *surahs*. While the rights and duties of men and women in society are touched on in the various *surahs*, *Surat-un-Nisa* ('The revelation about women'), the fourth *surah,* is dedicated solely to women. The translation of the Quran from the Arabic into English and Urdu is much contested by the various discourse communities because interpretations resonate in the national constitution and in the laws of the land. The process of interpreting sanctified texts is a major part of the hegemonic struggle. The traditionalists in Islamic societies derive legitimacy from their fundamentalist interpretation of Verse 34 in *Surat-un-Nisa*.

Interpretation of the Quran is, by definition, of any text a struggle for legitimacy and power. It is the manifestation of hegemony as process, the jostle within a 'lived system of meanings and values' (Williams, 1990, p. 110). Mailloux (1995) uses the terms 'interpretation'[16] and 'translation' almost interchangeably and informs that in Latin rhetoric, '*interpretatio* referred to the explanation of one word by another, the use of synonyms. *Interpretatio* was formed on *interpres*: "an intermediary, agent, go between" and an interpreter of foreign languages, a translator' (Glare, 1982, p. 947, as quoted in Mailloux 1995, p. 121). So, in translating and interpreting the various discourses and 'statements' (in the Foucauldian sense) that are connected to or seemingly connected to the phenomenon of honour killings, one has to be mindful of what Mailloux (1995) calls the two directions in which 'interpretation' conveys the sense of translation simultaneously: '*towards* a text to be interpreted and *for* an audience in need of the interpretation' (p. 121).

As an example of how subtly a seemingly harmless choice of words can change the spirit of the text, I am producing the translation of a contentious verse from the Quran by Mohammad Marmaduke William Pickthall (1875–1936), the son of a London clergyman who converted to Islam in 1917. Apart from becoming a leading Muslim cleric of his time, Pickthall edited the *Bombay Chronicle* for four years. A scholar of repute and a writer of several works of fiction, he considered his translation of the Quran his real lifetime achievement. In parentheses with the Pickthall text, I am interposing key words from the text of a translation by the eminent Islamic scholar Abul A'alaa Maududi. This juxtaposition highlights the significant shifts in meaning with the choice of words in the process of translating. Because the reader brings his/her own experience to the text which must be taken into account, that becomes a part of the inherent condition of the ongoing interpretive enterprise. Valery (1958) contends that:

> There is no true meaning to a text—no author's authority. Whatever he may have wanted to say, he has written what he has written. Once published, a text is like an apparatus that anyone may use as he will and according to his ability: it is not certain that the one who constructed it can use it better than another. (p. 152)

As history has amply demonstrated, these alleged and real differences in the strands of meaning in 'Divine' texts, the conflicting interpretations, have the potential to spawn sects within the belief system. The several major sects and sub-sects of Islam are constantly struggling (sometimes in bloody feuds)[17] for hegemony and claiming their interpretation to be *the* one that God meant. Here is the Pickthall translation of Verse 34, *Surah* 4 interspersed with Maududi's (1976) choice of English words for the same Arabic ones:

> Men are in charge of women (*men are the managers of the affairs of women*), because Allah has made one of them to excel (*superior to*) the other, and because they spend (*men spend of their wealth on women*) of their property (*for the support of women*). So good women are the obedient, guarding in secret that which Allah hath guarded (*Virtuous women are, therefore, obedient; they guard their rights carefully in their absence under the care and watch of Allah*). As for those from whom ye fear rebellion (*whose defiance you have cause to fear*), admonish them and banish them to beds apart, and scourge them (*keep them apart from your beds and beat them*). Then if they obey you (*submit to you*), seek not a way against them (*do not look for excuses to punish them*). Lo! Allah is ever High Exalted, Great (*note it well that there is Allah above you, who is Supreme and Great*). (p. 84)

Contextualizing the verse, the Muslim feminist Hassan (1994) takes issue with the Arabic word 'Qawwamun.' While the literalist translations put it as 'ruler' which in her view is akin to setting up a hierarchy, in her more egalitarian exegesis, Hassan (1994) argues to look at the men's function of supporting women in the context of child-bearing. The text intends to ensure that during child-bearing times women are taken care of properly without having to worry about the additional responsibilities of earning a living. The roles of men and women, as can be seen, are thus reversed. In this contextualized exegesis, not only are men not the rulers but are placed in the service of women. The Quran does not support the view that women were created from man or for man (see also Jawad, 1998). In this context, Engineer (1992) brings out another pertinent point by reflecting the social situation of the time when women did not generate material resources. In his view, it is important to note that the Quran does not say that men *should be* the *qawwamun* (which in his view means 'maintainers') but that men *are qawwamun.* If the Quran had said that men *should be qawwamun,* only then could it have been considered a normative statement binding on women for all ages and circumstances.

Because the above is a key verse that the orthodoxy use as evidence for Quranic injunction about male superiority, it needs a little more discussion. First, it is useful to understand the context of the revelation. Engineer (1992) suggests, on the authority of the noted Islamic commentator Zamakhshari, that an influential Muslim contemporary of the Prophet, Saad bin Rabi, slapped his wife, Habibah binte Zaid, because she disobeyed him. She complained to the Prophet through her father who was an influential man. The Prophet asked her to slap her husband back. This judgment outraged his contemporary men who were historically used to slave-like subservience by their women. It was in this context that the above *surah* was revealed to the Prophet. By today's standards it seems iniquitous to women, but really does not go beyond permitting the men to chastise their disobedient wives. According to Engineer (1992):

> Maybe the Prophet realized that his advice would have created an uproar in a society where man was completely dominant. The verse was revealed as soothing advice to control the violence of man towards woman and advising them to adjust themselves in a man-dominated society. (p. 47)

To appropriate such rhetoric for the purposes of killing women of one's family to address issues of honour is a huge leap. The Quran, as a revolutionary text, bestowed equality on females with males as no other divine text had done till then. According to Hassan (1994) 'An analysis of the Quranic descriptions of human creation shows how the Quran even-handedly uses both feminine and masculine terms and imagery to describe the creation of humanity from a single source' (p. 5). In different places, the text proclaims clear injunctions such as 'God's creation as a whole is for just ends' (Surah 15: Al-Hijr: 85) and not 'for idle sport' (Surah 21: Al-Anbiya: 16); that humanity consists of both man and woman 'in the best of moulds' (Surah 95: Al-Teen). In Hassan's (1994) view:

Not only does the Quran make it clear that man and woman stand absolutely equal in the sight of God, but also that they are 'members' and 'protectors' of each other. In other words, the Quran does not create a hierarchy in which men are placed above women nor does it pit men against women in an adversary relationship. They are created as equal creatures of a universal, just and merciful God whose pleasure it is that they live in harmony and righteousness. (p. 9)

As mentioned above, such differentiating interpretations of sanctified texts can spawn a variety of sects in systems of faith. The proliferation of churches, synagogues, and mosques of different denominations attests to the fact. It was the inevitability of divergent interpretations in any such enterprise that the Prophet Muhammad had in mind when he anticipated that there would be seventy-three different sects in Islam.[18] I hazard a guess that the Prophet used the number metaphorically for whatever the rhetorical punch of that number was at that time. The number of sects in Islam at the dawn of the twenty-first century is more than just that with some refusing to accept certain others as even Muslims.[19] None of those sects, however, presents an interpretation of the Quran where honour killing is even remotely condoned.

POLITICAL AND CIVIL SOCIETY IN PAKISTAN

It was important to delve into these texts and their interpretations of the Quran because the Constitution of Pakistan derives its legitimacy from the principles laid out by Islam. With a Muslim population of 97 percent, it follows that all political parties in Pakistan not only claim allegiance to Islam but also consider their interpretation to have ascendancy over all other interpretations. Thus, it is no surprise that the Constitution of Pakistan, deriving its legitimacy from the sacred Islamic texts passed by the national assembly in 1973, was endorsed by all political parties. The constitution is the fountainhead of powerful discourse communities such as the judiciary, the police, and other bureaucracies. This constitutes what Gramsci (1998) called the political society, the direct means of control of the polity. In Pakistani society the neighbourhood mosque represents an institution of voluntary affiliation that is not coercive but is no less powerful in influencing the public. For most of the people in Pakistan, the Friday sermon by the preacher is of fundamental importance in the conduct of their daily lives. This, in Gramscian terms, constitutes the civil society. All revolutions are predicated on the fact that the civil society may not have the legal punch of the political society, but is no less powerful. If the Berlin Wall represented the political dimension of the struggle for hegemony then the pieces of its rubble—now lying as souvenirs in some living rooms and museums of the world—bespeak the power of the civil society.

In Pakistani society, the views of the feminists and representatives of other groups—such as Human Rights Watch and Amnesty International, etc.—that are made available to the public through the media are also a part of the civil society. If the pulpit represents the traditional discourse, the feminists and modernists argue for reform in those traditions according to the changing times. Without taking issue with the religious texts, they debate the interpretations. Both constituents of the civil society want the attention of the political society and try to sway it in their direction. While the feminists and liberal activists, representing the rational mode of awareness, argue for the State to punish honour killing as any other murder, the traditionalists, representing the mythic awareness, plead for extenuating circumstances.

In the instance of Samia's murder, which became an intensely divisive issue between the two discursive formations, the traditionalists in what Irfani (23 August 1999) called 'a shocking inversion of values,' issued death threats to Samia's lawyers. These death threats were chanted in the streets and had the support of the mullahs because 'such demonstrations were backed by religious fatwas[20] calling on believers to kill Jilani and Jahangir as a religious duty.' A number of commentators emphasized how the proceedings in the Senate about Samia's killing signified a shift in the political ethos in the country, a change in the hegemonic configuration. Irfani (23 August 1999) was of the view that,

The Senate's silence on honour killings symbolizes a moral regression and cultural failure whose proportions are becoming increasingly frightening. After all, many of those who spearheaded the case for honour killing in the Senate once belonged to a political tradition known for its progressive and secular outlook.

All these shifts in alliances send messages to the outside world about the confusion in values and the direction that the country is headed. Additionally, such instances are messages to the citizens about the kind of behaviour that may be punished or tolerated. On the eve of the Senate proceedings about the resolution, Ziauddin (8 May 1999) wondered, 'what kind of signal would the Senate be sending to the law breakers in the country and to the world outside if they failed to condemn a murder.'

The next day the resolution was killed by creating legal obstacles by the senators from Samia's province in an alliance with those of the religious parties. One commentator, Musalman (19 September 1999), noted bemusedly the role of Wasim Sajjad, the Senate chair. A Rhodes Scholar and a brilliant legal mind, Sajjad is generally considered a liberal with his soft manner, and had usually voted for egalitarian causes. On this day, he buckled under pressure and used his powers to support the killing of the resolution, thus supporting the tribal custom. This was an example of the rational buckling under pressure from the mythic. Mussalman (19 September 1999) noted that: 'The dexterity of Chairman Wasim Sajjad, a jurist by training and profession, to help kill the resolution is indeed highly laudable.' Of note, of course, is the sarcasm of applauding the 'dexterity' rather than the 'belief,' the service to sophistry against essential goodness. Musalman also noted the tension between the power of the tradition and that of law: 'If discretionary traditional and tribal codes are the last word, then what is the fun of raising and maintaining the edifice of the judiciary.' Bari (as quoted in Amnesty International, September·1999) commented: 'It is highly unfortunate that the so-called custodians of the constitutional rights of the citizens are violating the constitution by upholding and reinforcing archaic tribal value systems, chauvinism, fanaticism, and political expediency' (p. 21).

SUMMARY

In this chapter I discussed the dispersion and configuration of power in the various discourse communities in Pakistan. Unfortunately, until now, when a cataclysmic incident such as the killing of a woman occurred for the sake of honour it went largely unnoticed. Representatives of certain communities, however, have a greater stake in how the State views the act. Women existing on the fringes of the society, in far-flung villages, without access to law or help from fellow urban women are the worst affected. As demonstrated by the Sindhi girl's poem, they live in perpetual fear of being violated and/or killed. These women, I argued, represent a different strand of feminism in Pakistan than the trained and suave professional women of the urban centres. Borrowing from Gramsci (1998) and Spivak (1998), I saw them as the subaltern(s) who may be comparatively feeble, but in their own way (and inevitably) they too interrupt the hegemonic discourse.

I looked at the judiciary as a key discourse community and a critical one in articulating and sending messages to the citizenry about which conduct is condoned and which is punished. For this, I presented certain judgments in cases of honour killing in which, in spite of their perspectival legal training, the judges felt compelled to take a lenient view of killings. This demonstrated the mythic dimension in their way of making sense of life. Further, I parsed certain key Quranic texts in order to understand the Islamic view of women and how the traditional, the mythic, is forever obliged to co-opt the religious texts to serve their ends. The discussion and the split in the Pakistan Senate about the notions of 'tradition' provided us with a prism to view the impossibility of placing people in sharply defined discourse communities or Gramscian classes.

NOTES

1. According to Patel (1991), 'Under the Draft Ordinance relating to *Qisas*... prepared by the Council of Islamic Ideology, *Qisas* means punishment by causing similar hurt to the offender' (p. 268).

2. According to Patel (1991), *Diyat* means 'Blood money or compensation for murder or man-slaughter. [It is the] compensation specified under the law payable to the heirs of the victim by the convict' (p. 264).

3. Moula Bux vs. the State, PCR LJ (p. 1752), p. 56 of the Amnesty International report.

4. Khanan Khan vs. the State, PCR LJ 1993, p. 56 of the Amnesty International report.

5. Muhammad Sharif vs. the State, 1983 Pcr LJ 1817; p. 57 of Amnesty International report.

6. According to Ashcroft, Griffiths, & Tiffin (1999), 'Subaltern, meaning "of inferior rank," is a term coined by Gramsci to refer to those groups in society who are subject to the hegemony of the ruling classes' (p. 215). Importantly, according to Gramsci (1998), 'The history of subaltern social groups is necessarily fragmented and episodic. There undoubtedly does exist a tendency toward (at least provisional stages of) unification in the historical activity of these groups, but this tendency is continually interrupted by the activity of the ruling groups ... subaltern groups are always subject to the activity of ruling groups, even when they rebel and rise up' (pp. 54–55). In the context of South Asia, 'subaltern' is used in Subaltern Studies according to Guha (1982), 'as a name for the general attribute of subordination in South Asian society whether this is expressed in terms of class, caste, age, gender, office, or in any other way' (p. vii).

7. I discuss the same poem in detail in the following chapter.

8. I borrow the term from Warhol and Herndl (1996) and deal with it in some detail a little later.

9. Spivak (1988) explains: 'The archival, historiographic, disciplinary-critical, and, inevitably, interventionist work involved here is indeed a task of "measuring silences"' (p. 286).

10. Although these words are often used synonymously, Said (1993) offers the following distinction between imperialism and colonialism: '"Imperialism" means the practice, the theory, and the attitudes of a dominating metropolitan centre ruling a distant territory; "colonialism," which is almost always a consequence of imperialism, is the implanting of settlements on distant territory' (p. 8).

11. Historiography means an accounting for different perspectives on writing history. According to Vitanza (1996), 'Historiography, in general, is the study of the different biases of, or attitudes toward, writing history...The

central question is one of whose interests, in a given history, are being served and whose are being deflected or forgotten' (p. 324).

12. Because 'Selections from the prison notebooks' was written often in codes (to get around the censors) the difficulties in translation and editing have been compounded. The footnote explaining the difficulty of translating and interpreting what Gramsci meant from *dirigere* and *egomania* runs to three fine printed pages. One has to defer to his interpretations of his work.

13. The sectarian strife, in Pakistan, is an 'on again, off again' phenomenon. During the late 1990s, hundreds of *Shias* (that comprise about 15 per cent of the Pakistani population) were killed. Some prominent ones were executed contract style. Of course, *Shias* also killed many *Sunnis* in retaliation. For the purposes of being in power, these disparate elements have now joined hands in an anti-American coalition in the post 9/11 world.

14. For detailed discussion, see chapter 5.

15. Senator Khattak had used the Arabic term *Naamoos* that is used for the honour of religious belief or with reference to the Prophet Muhammad or his *Sunnah*. Being a God term, *Namoos* would have had obvious resonance with the masses—Khattak's secondary audience and constituency for whom his message was *really* intended.

16. According to Mailloux (1995), the root word for 'interpretation' is the Latin *interpretatio* which means not only 'the action of expounding, explaining' but also 'translation, rendering.' In English usage, according to the Oxford English Dictionary (1985, p. 415), 'interpret' means to expound the meaning of (something abstruse or mysterious); to render (words, writings, an author) clear or explicit; to elucidate; to explain.' But the OED goes on to emphasize, 'Formerly, also, To translate (now only contextually, as included in the general sense).'

17. The constant sectarian strife in Pakistan is an example of this. During the 1991 and, then, 2003 Iraq war, Saddam Hussain, the Iraqi president, was constantly accused of brutally oppressing the majority Shiite population in Iraq.

18. Cited by Abou Dawood in *Hadith* #471.

19. The brutal persecution of the Bahais in Iran is an example. The Ahmedis, too, have been denied by the state in Pakistan to call themselves Muslims. Ironically, this was passed into law by the ostensibly modernist/secular Zulfikar Ali Bhutto under pressure from the religious zealots.

20. A word from the Islamic lexicon made familiar to the Westerners during the furor over Rushdie's (1989) *Satanic Verses, fatwa* is defined by Patel (1991) as 'a religious or judicial sentence/opinion pronounced by the *Khalifah* or by a *Mufti*, or *Qazi*. It is generally written' (p. 265).

7

Conclusion

Threshing out the metaphor of the 'silenced centre' (Mechery, 1978) again in conclusion, I admit the impossibility of measuring the depths and decibels of silences in the Pakistani society in which women are sacrificed at the altar of their men's honour. However, as was pointed out at the outset of this effort, the purpose of this study was an understanding of the phenomenon and not making claims or imposing ideologies. To this end, I put my ear to that 'silenced centre' and tried to absorb the situation as much as I could. Rather than claiming to present the exact measures, I have tried to diffuse the resonance of those silences, to disseminate the voice of those silences.

As I said at the outset, I am not an apologist for honour killing. On the contrary, it was because of the initial reflexive revulsion that I felt about the custom when I first read about it that I undertook the study. The purpose of this study was to develop an understanding of honour killing as a rhetorical move, a message in the communicative milieu of Pakistan. As a discipline, one of the functions of communication is to look at the ways people construct meaning, how they make sense of their daily lives. For this purpose, people send and receive messages within their families and to the representatives of outside social institutions. Honour killing is a powerful message. It is a phenomenon worthy of study: What makes people put an abstraction such as honour before something as concrete as the life of someone they love most?

The ways honour killing—as a message—is received, understood, and responded to by the various discourse communities that constitute Pakistan has been the focus of the study. Borrowing the conceptualizations of 'hegemony,' 'subaltern,' 'power,' and 'discourse communities' from Gramsci, Foucault, Spivak, etc., I looked at the representative texts of the various groups in order to understand how they perceive the act of honour killing. Embedded in the texts are the ways power, gender, religion, rights, duties, and violence are viewed by the discourse communities (see also Coates, 1986). The data for the study came from texts of newspaper articles, recorded speeches, senate hearings, reports of organizations, personal interviews, and other sources, as written or spoken messages of activists, lawyers, religious scholars, preachers, senators, judges, and representative citizens of Pakistan. These texts provided insight into why the traditionalist discursive community considers its customs under assault from 'pollution importers' and the vehemence and vigour with which they defend their traditions. The texts also, however, illuminated the fear and anger of women faced with honour killing, and their attempts at acquiring agency.

Gebser's (1985) theory of consciousness development or shifts in structures of awareness and Kramer's (1997) theory of dimensional accrual/dissociation provided a prism to view the resurgence in honour killing in Pakistan as a manifestation of the interface between the mythic and the mental realms. The tribal, the conventional, the local, the traditional, code of conduct, and such were all terms utilized in the various discourses as epitomes of the mythic, while modern, education, foreign, NGOs, Human Rights, feminisms and such represented the mental mode of awareness. According to Kramer (1997), 'As dimensional awareness accrues, so too dissociation increases' (p. xiii). While in the mythic mode of being, identity is not as collectivistic as in the magic mode, dissociation is not as extreme as it is in the mental, where, with the accrual of the third dimension, emotional detachment is increased. In present-day Pakistan, there exists a strong mythic realm as is evidenced by practices such as honour killing. At the same time, Pakistan is marching toward modernity with its concomitant atomism and dissociation. Thus, there is a tension and a crisis of identity and values. It is at the interface of the mythic and the mental that the discussion around honour killing has erupted. For some honour killing is a *cause celebre*, a defining aspect of their collective identity; for others it is a barbaric practice of a tribal mindset with little relevance to the present time.

In my view honour killing, wherever it is perpetrated, belongs to the mythic realm. It is not rational behaviour; it does not belong to the mental. Neither is it a reflexive, knee-jerk, thoughtless, enraged spilling of blood as happens in crimes of passion. That belongs to the magical where the identity of the individual is one with the universe. Compelled by mythologized cultural notions about identity, honour, gender, power, masculinity and so on, some men feel duty bound to kill. Honour killing is a manifestation of a deficient and exhausted attitude mired in the mythic past. The embedded mythic is colliding with emergent rational modes of awareness in Pakistan.

In a cruel irony, the victims of honour killing are more important to, and more loved by, the perpetrator of the crime than by outsiders, yet it is the outsiders who find the practice reprehensible. Within the society, the perpetrator is often applauded. He, too, is a member of a society partially mired in archaic modes of awareness and views of masculinity. My purpose was to recreate, as much as I could, the semiotic universe in which the sway of such hegemonic masculinity triggers honour killing as a message.

Honour killing is a primal act and knows no religions, cultural, racial, or geographical boundaries. Most ancient legal codes—including Hammurabi, the oldest one extant—have conceded the right to offended husbands to divorce, torture, or even kill their wives. Likewise, pre-Islamic Arabs did not allow for rights of women. Womanhood was a stigma to the extent that in most of the tribes in the Arabian Peninsula daughters were buried alive at their birth. It is difficult to measure the success of a religion but, like all religions, Islam appeared as a civilizing force on a brutal cultural landscape. Islam provided structure, dignity, hope, and a way of life to warlike nomadic people. More relevantly to this work, Islam provided equality to women.

For hermeneutics to yield any meaningful understanding, one must consider the inescapability of sociological influence while interpreting divine scriptures. It is not a question of honesty. Rather, it is the acceptance of the polysemic possibilities of language over space and time. Thus, the more orthodox interpretations[1] from the sacred texts about women's veils, etc., at the service of the mythic realm should be understood in that context. It is not different from the justification of slavery in both Christianity and Islam through the sacred texts by scholars of earlier times. According to Engineer (1992), Muslim jurists, citing authority from exact language of the Quran, continued to justify slavery throughout the European Middle Ages. To own slaves was considered a God-given right just like owning property or, as some orthodoxies would have us believe, women. A slave who ran away from his master was regarded as a sinner and interpretations of the Quranic injunctions were presented as authority. In certain 'Islamic' societies, women's struggle for independence and dignity has been and is being resisted with similar discourses. Honour killing is simply an extreme redress by men who interpret the sacred texts according to their tribal vision of life.

Every epoch has its intellectual and moral climate. Interpretations of the sacred texts are inevitably affected by it. The Islamic theologians of the first century[2] whose opinions are much regarded to this day and who compiled the *ahadith* were also subject to sociological influences. Technically converted to Islam, those theologians were still psychologically and socially mired in the pre-Islamic attitudes about women when women were viewed as little more than chattel; as instruments to provide males for the clan, bring up those males, and provide pleasure to their husbands. These attitudes are reflected in those interpretations and to this day remain the 'guiding light' for the orthodoxy.

It should be noted that one of the principles of Islamic scholarship is *ijtihad* (exertion).[3] It encourages the creative interpretation and application of Islamic *fiqh* (jurisprudence) in the face of emerging realities. According to Engineer (1992), 'The principle of *ijtihad*, so long as it was applied, constituted a dynamic element in Islamic law. Unfortunately, the gates of *ijtihad* were closed soon after the decline of the Abbasid empire in the 12th century A.D.' (p. 6). Incidentally, that was the time of the vibrant blossoming of Islamic intellectual tradition that, through the works of Ibn Rushd (Avirroes), Ibn Sina (Avicenna), Ibn Hizm, etc., was the precursor to the European Renaissance. In modern-day Pakistan, women have to be granted their due dignity and rights in the light of fresh interpretations (*ijtihad*) of the sacred texts.

Additionally, for these ends, men have to make adjustments in their social roles and their expectations from women. In due course, they need to be culturally trained to come to terms with a view of masculinity that is more in tune with the emerging global ethos and not mired in ancient tribal myths. The challenges to what Connell (2002) calls 'gender order' (p. 249) by women should be taken into account. Societies, then, can be organized in the emerging new ways. Through a variety of political movements, women in the West have challenged men's prerogatives for more than a century. According to Connell (2002) 'The conditions for the maintenance of patriarchy changed with these challenges, and the kind of masculinity which could be hegemonic changed in response' (p. 250).

Education for the awareness of human rights and equality has to be cross-gender: if women are to be empowered, men have to be alerted to adjust their roles and identities. Islam provides a way out of this gender identity crisis in Pakistan with its emphasis on *ijtihad*. The symbolic definition of masculinity drenched in violence and propagated by the bearers of the fundamentalist agenda in the political fray of Pakistan can be neutralized only from within, i.e., the re-interpretations of the sacred texts. Justice Jilani (1999) of the Pakistan High Court was making this point when he stated that the culture in Pakistan is being influenced by prejudices bequeathed by history, tradition, and feudalism, and this needs to be tamed by law informed by an objective understanding of Islamic laws. Jilani (1999) said, 'Male chauvinism, feudal bias, and compulsions of a conceited ego should not be confused with Islamic values' (p. 49). Men have to learn that 'male' and 'masculinity' are different things. As Connell (1995) puts it 'Masculinity is planted in the male body, it does not grow out of it' (p. 126). To expunge the practice of *karo kari* (honour killing) from the cultural landscape of Pakistan, it is not only the women who need to be educated and empowered, but the men must be infused with a less hegemonic and more harmonic vision of masculinity.

Discussing fascism and other violent upheavals in recent history, Connell (2002) brings up a point extremely relevant to the situation in Pakistan:

> In gender terms, fascism was a naked aggression of male supremacy in societies that had been moving towards equality for women. To accomplish this, fascism promoted new images of hegemonic masculinity, glorifying irrationality (the 'triumph of the will,' thinking with 'the blood') and the unrestrained violence of the frontier soldier. Its dynamics soon led to a new and even more devastating global war. (p. 250)

For me, the parallels of the rise of fascism in Europe and the rise of similar 'thinking with the blood' movements in Pakistan are stark, eerie, and frightening. Starting with neighbouring Afghanistan, in Pakistan, too, the apocalyptic self-righteous vision of the Taliban and the Al-Qaeda is in the process of brutally trampling the innocent steps taken by the nascent feminist movements. There is news of vigilante groups of young men who march to a martial beat in the streets and bazaars rudely yelling at decent women to conduct themselves in their (mythic) version of modesty. Alarmingly, there have been incidents of acid-throwing at women who were not 'properly' veiled. It was under the banner of these new images of 'hegemonic masculinity' that men intimidated the judiciary and other national institutions to view, among other things, cases of honour killing in their traditional ways. Such blazing visions have to be neutralized by an internal light rather than from the outside pulverizing by Stealth Bombers and Drones which, apart from creating untold misery, have the potential to create 'new and improved' monsters mutated from their Taliban and Al-Qaeda ancestors.

LIMITATIONS AND FUTURE DIRECTIONS

There were several limitations to this research project. The project started as an attempt to understand the phenomenon of honour killing in certain human societies. From the initial readings it quickly became clear that it is not confined to Pakistan or a few other societies, but that women have been (and are) killed by their men for a variety of reasons all over the globe. Taking into account, for the purposes of this work, the variety of cultures from the Indian subcontinent to the Mediterranean, from the Christian to the Islamic, and from Italy to the Far East—some of the areas where honour killing has been evidenced—could not have been possible with the time and resources available. Discovering such scale to be beyond the scope of this project, I narrowed the definition of honour killing and brought my focus into Pakistan. Even in Pakistan several distinct cultures[4] thrive, each with its own history and justification for the act. But Islam and Pakistan provide an anchoring commonality of religion and nationality that provided me with a way to view them in the same sweep. One area that future research on honour killing can explore is the comparison between Muslim and other societies, such as Christian. Jewish, and Hindu, where honour killing is practiced. While there is evidence that the practice continues to some degree in certain Latin American and Mediterranean countries, there is no denying that it is more common in certain Muslim countries. The few cases of honour killing in Europe too have occurred in Muslim immigrant families. The interesting question for future research to explore can be about the persistence of such crimes in Islamic societies in spite of clear injunctions in Islamic sacred texts against all vigilante responses to real or perceived breaches of personal or collective honour.

There were two main limitations to this research. The first, and the more intractable one, was the unprecedented political turmoil in the area. Pakistan, especially the region close to Afghanistan, has been described as the most dangerous and volatile in the world since 9/11. With the eruption of hostilities, people's political positions and religious beliefs have become hardened. Relatedly, they have become apprehensive about their future and suspicious about strangers. During my trips I felt an ominous mix of hopelessness and jingoism that hung in the air. On the one hand, educated people in urban areas, especially political activists, were too keen to be heard. Meanwhile in rural areas, where most of the honour killings take place, people eyed me suspiciously. I tried to gain access to families who have experienced honour killing but, in the existing political climate, it was not possible. In my view, interviews, especially with women, in rural areas could have shed useful light.

Also, because of the heightened security considerations, I could not interview anyone who may have committed honour killing and was serving time. That point of view is important, too. In a different political climate, future research could be enriched from those insights and by the opinions of a perpetrator of honour killing. Another rich source of data might be an ethnography of court proceedings about such cases. It would be interesting to note the language in which the crime was justified and the court's view about it. This is where the second limitation affected the research. I did find cases lined up for hearings, but none came up for hearing during my visits to Pakistan. I found rulings by lower courts on some cases of honour killing and have presented those as evidence of the way the judiciary as the law-imposing arm of the State typically views such crimes. Future research could certainly benefit from actual ethnographies of court proceedings rather than making do with the transcripts of rulings.

NOTES

1. And mythologizing, I may add, as we saw in the oratorical flourishes of Faisalabadi.
2. I mean the Islamic calendar, which started in AD 622.
3. According to Patel (1991) 'Maududi has defined *ijtihad* as an academic research and intellectual effort which makes the legal system of Islam dynamic and its development and evolution in the changing times possible' (p. 104).
4. The Pathans of the north and northwest mountains, for example, speak an entirely different language (Pushto) than the desert dwelling Sindhis (who speak Sindhi). The geographical distance and climate also contribute to their different ethnic character.

Bibliography

Abu-Odeh, L. (1996). Crimes of honour and the construction of gender in Arab societies. In M. Yamani (Ed.), *Feminism and Islam: Legal and literary perspectives* (pp. 141–194). New York: New York University Press.

Ahmed, L. (1992). *Women and gender in Islam.* New Haven, CT: Yale University Press.

Ahmed, N. (7 September 1999). Honour Killing: A legacy or heritage? *The News.*

Abdul Baqi, M.F. (Ed.). (1945). *Al Muajjam Al Mufahris Le Alfaaz Al Quran Al Karim* (xxth ed.). Beirut: Muassisa Manabil Al Irfan.

Ali, T. (2002). Mullahs and heretics. [Electronic version]. *London Review of Books*, 24(3), 1–21.

Amnesty International. (September 1999). *Pakistan: Violence against women in the name of honour.* (AI Index: ASA 33/17/99). London.

AI [Amnesty International] launches campaign against 'honour killings.' (22 September 1999). *The News.*

Anderson, J.A. (1996a). *Communication Theory: Epistemological foundations.* New York: The Guilford Press.

Anderson, J.A. (1996b). Thinking qualitatively: Hermeneutics in science. In M. Salwen & D. Stacks (Eds.), *An integrated approach to communication theory and research* (pp. 45–59). Mahwah, NJ: Lawrence Earlbaum.

Aristotle (1954). *Rhetoric and poetics.* New York: The Modern Library.

Ashcroft, B., Griffiths, G., & Tiffin, H. (1999). *Key concepts in post-colonial studies.* London: Routledge.

Baker, N.V., Gregware, P.R., & Cassidy, M.A. (1999). Family killing fields: Honour rationales in the murder of women. *Violence against women*, 5(2), 164–184.

Bakhtin, M. (1986). *Speech genres and other late essays.* In Caryl Emerson & Michael Holoquist (Eds.). Austin: University of Austin Press.

Bakhtin, M. (1998). From *Discourse in the novel.* In David Richter (Ed.) *The critical tradition: Classic texts and contemporary trends.* Boston: Bedford Books.

Baolbaki, R. (Ed.). (1995). *Al Mawrid Al Quareeb: An Arabic-English dictionary* (Xth ed.). Beirut: Dar El-lim Lilmalayin.

Barthes, R. (1989). *Mythologies*. New York: Noonday Press.

Benjamin, W. (1968). *Illuminations*. New York: Schocken Books.

Bourdieu, P. (1970). The sentiment of honour in Kabyle society. In J.G. Peristiany (Ed.), *Honour and shame: The values of Mediterranean society*. Chicago: The University of Chicago Press.

Brodsky, J. (1986). *Less than one: Selected essays*. New York: Farrar Straus Giroux.

Burke, K. (1954). *A grammar of motives*. New York: Prentice-Hall.

Campbell, J.K. (1964). *Honour, family, and patronage: A study of institutions and moral values in a Greek mountain community*. London: Oxford University Press.

Cantarella, E. (1991). Homicides of honour: The development of Italian adultery law over two millennia. In D. Kertzer & R.P. Saller (Eds.), *The family in Italy: From antiquity to the present* (pp. 229–244). New Haven: Yale University Press.

Coates, J. (1986). *Women, men, and language: A sociolinguistic account of sex differences in language*. New York: Longman.

Cohen, D. (1991). The Augustan law on Adultery: The social and cultural context. In D.K. & R.P. Saller (Eds.), *The family in Italy: from antiquity to the present* (pp. 109–126). New Haven: Yale University Press.

Connell, B. (1995). Masculinity, violence, and war. In M. Kimmel & M. Messner, (Eds.), *Men's lives* (pp. 125–130). Needham Heights, MA: Allyn & Bacon.

Connell, R. (2002). The history of masculinity. In R. Adams & D. Savran (Eds.), *The masculinities studies reader* (pp. 245–261). Malden, MA: Blackwell Publishers.

Cowasjee, A. (9 March 2003). Blackened woman, blackened man. *Dawn*.

Dawood, A. (1999). Karo-kari: A question of honour, but whose honour? *Feminista 2*, 3–4.

de Certeau, M. (1984). *The practice of everyday life* (S. Rendall, Trans.). Berkeley: University of California Press.

Ede, L., Glenn, C., & Lunsford, A. (1995). Border crossings: Intersections of rhetoric and feminism. *Rhetorica, 4*, 401–443.

Engineer, A. (1992) *The rights of women in Islam*. Delhi, India: Sterling Publishers.

Fagles, R., & Stanford, W. (1982). A reading of the Oresteia: The serpent and the eagle. In Robert Fagles (Ed. and Trans.). *Aeschylus: The Oresteia*. New York: Bantam.

Faisalabadi, Q. (2002). Sound recording. Bagh Sardaaraan, Rawalpindi: Tableeghi Islami Cassette Center.

Faqir, F. (2001). Intrafamily femicide in defense of honour: The case of Jordan. *Third World Quarterly, 22* (1), 65-82.

Feroze, S.M.A. (2001). *Urdu-English Dictionary*. Lahore: Caravan Press.

Fontana, A., & Frey, J. H. (2000). The interview: From structured questions to negotiated text. In N.K. Denzin & Y.S. Lincoln (Eds.), *Handbook of qualitative research* (pp. 645–672). Thousand Oaks, CA: Sage Publications.

Foss, S.K., Foss, K.A., & Trapp, R. (1991). *Contemporary perspectives on rhetoric*. Prospect Heights, IL: Waveland Press, Inc.

Foucault, M. (1972). *The archaealogy of knowledge and the discourse on language*. New York: Pantheon.

Foucault, M. (1980). *Power/Knowledge: Selected interviews and other writings (1972–1977)*. New York, Pantheon.

Foucault, M. (1990). *The history of sexuality. Vol. 1: An introduction*. New York: Vintage Books.

Foucault, M. (1995). *Discipline and punish: The birth of the prison*. New York: Vintage.

Freeman, J.F. (1992). Gebser's understanding of political practice. In E. Kramer (Ed.), *Consciousness and culture: An introduction to the thought of Jean Gebser* (pp. 147–160). Westport, CT: Greenwood.

Freud, S. (1950). *Totem and taboo: Some points of agreement between the mental lives of savages and neurotics*. New York: W.W. Norton & Company.

Friedrich, P. (1977). Sanity and the myth of honour: The problem of Achilles. *Ethos, 5*, pp. 281–305.

Gadamer, H.G. (1976). *Philosophical hermeneutics*. (D. Linge, Trans.). Berkeley: University of California Press.

Gadamer, H.G. (1998a). *Truth and Method*. New York: Continuum.

Gadamer, H.G. (1998b). The elevation of the historicality of understanding of the status of hermeneutical principle. In D.H. Richter (Ed.), *The critical tradition: Classic texts and contemporary trends* (pp. 671-688). Boston: Bedford Books.

Galtung, J. (1990). Cultural violence. *Journal of peace research, 27(3)*, 291–305.

Gebser, J. (1985). *The ever present origin*. Athens, OH: Ohio University Press.

Geertz, C. (1973). *The interpretation of cultures*. New York: Basic Books.

Geertz, C. (1983). *Local knowledge: Further essays in interpretive anthropology*. New York: Basic Books.

Girard, R. (1977). *Violence and the sacred*. (P. Gregory, Trans.). Baltimore: The Johns Hopkins University Press.

Gramsci, A. (1998). *Selections from prison notebooks*. Hyderabad, India: Orient Longman.

Gubrium, J.F., & Holstein, J.A. (1998). Narrative practices and the coherence of personal stories. *Sociological Quarterly, 39*, 163-187.

Guha, R. (1982). *Subaltern Studies 1: Writings on South Asian history and society* (Vol. 7). Delhi: Oxford University Press.

Guillame, A. (1966). *The traditions of Islam*. Beirut: Khayats.

Haider, I. (10 September 1999). Silencing the Senate. *Dawn*.

Haider, I. (9 September 1999). Senate and the Samia case: The real story. *The News*.

Hall, E. (1969). *The hidden dimension*. Garden City, NJ: Anchor Books.

Hameed, A. (20 August 1999). Islam doesn't give anyone a license to kill. *Ausaf*, p. 8.

Hassan, R. (1994). *Women's rights and Islam: From the I.C.P.D to Beijing*. Unpublished manuscript.

Heidegger, M. (1962). *Being and time*. New York: Harper and Row.

Helsley, S. (1996). Kairos. In T. Enos (Ed.). *Encyclopedia of rhetoric and composition: Communication from ancient times to the information age* (p. 371). New York: Garland.

Hoffer, E. (1989). *The true believer: Thoughts on the nature of mass movements*. New York: Harper and Row.

Hoftstede, G. (1980). *Culture's consequences: International differences in work-related values*. Beverly Hills: Sage.

Hofstede, G. (1991). *Cultures and organizations: Software of the mind*. London: McGraw-Hill.

Hofstede, G. (2001). *Cultures consequences: Comparing values, behaviors, institutions, and organizations across nations*. New Delhi, India: Sage Publications.

Holstein, J. A., & Gubrium, J. F. (1995). *The active interview*. Thousand Oaks, CA: Sage.

Honour killings condemned. (19 August 1999). *The News*.

hooks, b. (1989). *Talking back: Thinking feminists, thinking black*. Boston: South End.

Hsu, F. (1971). Psychosocial homeostasis and jen: Conceptual tools for advancing psychological anthropology. *American Anthropologist, 73*, 23–44.

Hui, C., & Triandis, H. (1986). Individualism-Collectivism: A study of cross-cultural researchers. *Journal of Cross Cultural Psychology, 17*, 225–248.

Human Rights Commission of Pakistan. (2000, April). *Violence against women*. Vol. XI no. 4. (pp. 11–13). Lahore, Pakistan: Maktaba Jadeed Press.

Husain, I. (17 April 1999). Samia's 'crime' … and punishment. *Dawn*.

International Rural Development Program Report (IRDP). (1984–90). Retrieved 2 May 2003, from http://www.mardan.sdnpk.org/IRSP. htm

Irfani, S. (23 August 1999). Hostage to idols. *Dawn*.

Jahan, T. (January 1999). Faces of tyranny as mirrored in the press. *HRCP Newsletter, 10(1)*, Lahore: Maktaba Jadeed Press.

Jan, A. (24 August 1999). Don't let our honour die. *The Frontier Post*.

Jasam, S. (2000). *Honour killing in Pakistan*. Unpublished master's thesis, Institute of Social Science, The Hague, Netherlands.

Jawad, H.A. (1998). *The rights of women in Islam*. London: Macmillan Press.

Jilani, A. (21 March 1999). Honour amongst murderers. *Dawn*.

Jilani, T. (September 1999). Ruling in Humaira Khokhar case. *Amnesty International Report*, (AI Index: ASA 33/17/99). London.

Kamal, S., & Khan, A. (1997). *A study of the interplay of formal and customary laws on women. Vol. 1*. Lahore: Maktaba Jadeed.

Kandiyoti. D. (1987). Emancipated but unliberated? Reflections on the Turkish case. *Feminist Studies, 13*, 317–338.

Kapuscinski, R. (1994). *The Emperor and shah of shahs*. London: Picador.

Khan, T. (18 April 1999). Violence against women. *Dawn*.

Kincheloe, J., & McLaren, P. (2000). Rethinking critical theory and qualitative research. In N. Denzin & Y. Lincoln (Eds.), *Handbook of Qualitative Research*. New Delhi: Sage.

Kinneavy, J. (1980). *Theory of discourse*. New York: Norton.

Kramer, E.M. (1992). *Consciousness and culture: An introduction to the thought of Jean Gebser*. Westport, CT: Greenwood Press.

Kramer, E.M. (1997). *Modern/Postmodern: Off the beaten path of antimodernism*. Westport, CT: Praeger.

Kramer, E.M. (2000). Cultural fusion and the defense of difference. In M. Asante & J. E. Min (Eds.), *African-American and Korean-American relations* (pp. 183-230). New York: University Press of America.

Kramer, E. and Ikeda, R. (2001). Defining crime: Signs of postmodern murder and the "Freeze" case of Yoshiro Hattori. *The American Journal of Semiotics, 17,* 19–84.

Kramer, E. & Mickunas, A. (1992). Introduction: Gebser's new understanding. In E. Kramer (Ed.). *Conscious and culture: An introduction to the thought of Jean Gebser* (pp. xi–xxxi). Westport, CT: Greenwood Press.

Kramer, E. & Richiko, I. (1998). Understanding different worlds: The theory of dimensional accrual/dissociation. *Journal of Intercultural Communication, 2,* 37–51.

Kramer, S.N. (1963). *The Sumerians: Their history, culture, and character.* Chicago, IL: University of Chicago Press.

Kressel, G.M. (1981). Sororocide/Filiacide: Homicide for Family Honour: *Current Anthropology, 22 (2),* 141–158.

Kristeva, J. (1998). Psychoanalysis and the polis. In D. Richter (Ed.) *The critical tradition: Classic texts and contemporary trends* (pp. 1075–1086). Boston, MA: Bedford Books.

Lane, E. (1956). *An Arabic-English lexicon Book 1, Part 6.* Edinburg: Williams & Norgate.

Lang, S.D. (2000). *Sharaf politics: Constructing male prestige in Israeli-Palestinian society.* Unpublished doctoral dissertation, Harvard University, Cambridge.

Lears, J. (11 March 2003). How war became a crusade. *New York Times,* p. 25.

Lerner, G. (1986): *The creation of patriarchy.* New York: Oxford University Press.

Lofland, L., & Lofland, L. H. (1995). *Analyzing social settings: A guide to qualitative observation and analysis.* Belmont, CA: Wadsworth Publishing Company.

Mailloux, S. (1995). Interpretation. In F. Lentricchia & T. McLaughlin (Eds.), *Critical terms for literary study* (pp. 121–134). Chicago: The University of Chicago Press.

Malinowski, B. (1961). *Argonauts of the Western Pacific.* Prospect Heights, IL: Waveland Press, Inc.

Maududi, A. (1976). *The meaning of Quran.* Lahore: Islamic Publications.

Mechery, P. (1978). *A theory of literary production*. (G. Wall, Trans.). London: Routledge.

Mernissi, F. (1987). *Beyond the veil*. London: Al Saqi Books. OR Mernissi, F.

Mickunas, A. (1994). The terrible beauty and her reflective force. In K. Callaghan (Ed.). *Ideals of feminine beauty: Philosophical, social, and cultural dimensions* (pp. 3–19). Westport, CT: Greenwood Press.

Minces, J. (1982). *House of obedience: Women in Arab society*. London. Zed.

Murphy, J. (1997). The importance of social imagery for race relations. In E. M. Kramer (Ed.), *Postmodernism and race*, (pp. 17–29). Westport, CT: Greenwood.

Musalman, A.A. (19 September 1999). Honour killing: The killing of a resolution. *The News*.

Naqvi, A. (18 October 1999). *The News*.

Niazi, M. (7 May 1999). The state's tribal tragedy. *Dawn*.

Nietzsche, F. (1956). *The birth of tragedy & The geneology of morals* (Francis Golfing, Trans.). New York: Anchor Books.

Nietzsche, F. (1974). *The gay science* (Walter Kaufman, Trans.). New York: Vintage.

Ortner, S. (1978). The virgin and the state. *Feminist Studies, 4*, 19–35.

Palmer, P. (1969). *Hermeneutics: Interpretation theory in Schleiermacher, Dilthey, Heidegger, and Gadamer*. Evanston, IL: Northwestern University Press.

Patel, R. (1991). *Socio-economic political status and women and law in Pakistan*. Karachi, Pakistan: Faiza.

Pathan, N. (19 August 1991). Honour killings condemned. *The News*.

Patton, Q. P. (1990). *Qualitative evaluation and research methods*. Newbury Park, CA: Sage.

Paz, O. (1991). *The other voice: Essays on modern poetry*. Orlando, FL: Harcourt Brace Jovanovich.

Peristiany, J.G. (1970). Introduction. In J. G. Peristiany (Ed.), *Honour and shame: The values of Mediterranean society* (pp. 9–18). Chicago: The University of Chicago Press.

Pitt-Rivers, J. (1970). Honour and social status. In J.G. Persitiany (Ed.), *Honour and shame: The values of Mediterranean society* (pp. 21–77). Chicago: The University of Chicago Press.

Qasmi, A. (13 September 1999). A mother is a woman. *Daily Jang*, p. 3.

Radford, J. (1992). Introduction. In J. Radford & D. Russell (Eds.). *Femicide: The politics of women killing* (pp. iii–xii). New York: Twayne Publishers.

Reynolds, N. (1998). Interrupting our way to agency: Feminist cultural studies and composition. In S. Jarrat & L. Worshom, (Eds.). *Feminism and composition studies: In other words* (pp. 58–73). New York: The Modern Language Association of America.

Ricoeur, P. (1974). *The conflict of interpretations: Essays in hermeneutics.* Evanston: Northwestern University Press.

Ricoeur, P. (1976). *Interpretation Theory: Discourse and the surplus of meaning.* Fort Worth: Texas Christian University Press.

Ricoeur, P. (1987). *Hermeneutics and the human sciences.* (J.B. Thomson, Trans.) Paris: Cambridge University Press.

Said, E. (1993). *Culture and imperialism.* London: Chatto and Windus.

Said, E. (1998). From the Introduction to Orientalism. In D. Richter (Ed.), *The critical tradition: Classic texts and contemporary trends* (pp. 1279–1292). Boston: St. Martin's Press.

Scheurich, J. (1997). *Research method in the postmodern.* London: Falmer.

Schneider, J. (1971). Of vigilance and virgins: Honour, shame, and access to resources in Mediterranean societies. *Ethnology, 10,* 1–24.

Schwandt, T. (1997). *Qualitative Inquiry: A dictionary of terms.* Thousand Oaks, CA: Sage.

Schwartz, S., & Bilsky, W. (1990). Toward a theory of the universal content and structure of values. *Journal of Personality and Social Psychology, 58,* 878–891.

Senators oppose resolution condemning Samia's murder. (3 August 1999). *Dawn.*

Serhan, R. (1997). *Honour without women: Honour and the legitimization of murder in the criminal courts of Lebanon.* Unpublished Master's thesis, University of Windsor, Canada.

Shah, H. (1998). Reflections on the law of qisas and diyat. In *Shaping women's lives: Laws, practices, and strategies in Pakistan.* Lahore: Shirkatgah.

Shah, N. (19 November 1999). Honour Killing. *Dawn.*

Shaheed, F. (1998). Engagements of culture, customs, and law: Women's lives and activism. In *Shaping women's lives: Laws, practices, and strategies in Pakistan* (p. 70). Lahore: Shirkatgah.

Shahid, N. (12 April 1999). Victims of honour. *Dawn*.

Shakespeare, W. (1991). *The Sonnets*. New York: Gramercy Park Books.

Siddiqui, M. (June 1999). Murder of honour. *Muhaddis*, pp. 47–58.

Spivak, G. (1982). Translator's preface. In J. Derrida, *Of Grammatology* (pp. ix–xxxvii). Baltimore: Johns Hopkins Press.

Spivak, G. (1998). Can the subaltern speak? In C. Nelson & L. Grossberg (Eds.). *Marxism and the interpretation of culture* (pp. 271–313). Chicago: University of Illinois Press.

Stern, J. (2000). Pakistan's jehad culture. *Foreign Affairs, 79*, 115–120.

Ting-Toomey, S. (1994). Managing intercultural conflicts effectively. In L. Samovar & R. Porter (Eds.), *Intercultural communication: A Reader* (pp. 360–372). Belmont, CA: Wadsworth, Inc.

Tonnies, F. (1963/1887). *Community and society*. New York: Harper & Row.

Tresidder, J. (1997). *Dictionary of symbols: An illustrated guide to traditional images, icons, and* emblems. San Francisco: Chronicle Books.

Triandis, H. (1988). Collectivism and Individualism: A reconceptualization of a basic concept in cross-cultural social psychology. In G.K. Verma & C. Bagley (Eds.), *Cross cultural studies of personality, attitudes and cognition* (pp. 60–95). London: Macmillan.

Triandis, H. (1995). *Individualism and collectivism*. San Francisco: Westview Press.

Triandis, H., Brislin, R., & Hui, C. (1988). Cross-cultural training across the individualism-collectivism divide. *International Journal of Intercultural Relations, 12*, 269–289.

Verbatim Record of the Proceedings of the Senate (of Pakistan). 96th Session (10 May 1999), p. 32.

Vitanza, V. (1996). Historiographies of rhetoric. In T. Enos (Ed.). *Encyclopedia of rhetoric and composition: Communication from ancient times to the information age* (pp. 324–325). New York: Garland.

Walther, W. (1993). *Women in Islam*. New York: Markus Wiener Publishing.

Warhol, R. & Herndl, D. (1991). About *feminisms*. In R. Warhol & D. Herndl (Eds.), *Feminisms: An anthology of literary theory and criticism* (pp. ix–xvi). New Brunswick, NJ: Rutgers.

Weaver, R. (1953). *The ethics of rhetoric*. Chicago: Henry Regery.

Wheeler, L., Reis, H., & Bond, M. (1989). Collectivism-Individualism in everyday social life: The middle kingdom and the melting pot. *Journal of Personality and Social Psychology, 57*, 79–86.

Williams, R. (1985). *Keywords: A vocabulary of culture and society*. New York: Oxford University Press.

Williams, R. (1990). *Marxism and literature*. New York: Oxford University Press.

Young, D. (1992). *Origins of the sacred: The ecstasies of love and war*. New York: HarperPerrenial.

Yousufzai, I. (6 May 1990). Pukhtunwali—Rights and obligations. *Dawn*.

Yousufzai, R. (18 November 1999). Counter-accusations. *Dawn*.

Ziauddin, M. (8 May 1999). The legitimacy of honour killing. *Dawn*.

Index